with Blood and Fire

Life behind Union Lines in Middle Tennessee, 1863–65

Michael R. Bradley

Ours the Blood
Michael R Bradley

BURD STREET PRESS
SHIPPENSBURG, PENNSYLVANIA

This Burd Street Press publication
was printed by
Beidel Printing House, Inc.
63 West Burd Street
Shippensburg, PA 17257-0708 USA

The acid-free paper used in this book meets the guidelines for permanence and durability of the Committee on Production Guidelines for Book Longevity of the Council on Library Resources.

For a complete list of available publications
please write
Burd Street Press
Division of White Mane Publishing Company, Inc.
P.O. Box 708
Shippensburg, PA 17257-0708 USA

Library of Congress Cataloging-in-Publication Data

Bradley, Michael R. (Michael Raymond), 1940-
    With blood and fire : life behind Union lines in middle Tennessee, 1863-65 / Michael R. Bradley.
      p. cm.
    Includes bibliographical references and index.
    ISBN 1-57249-323-2 (alk. paper)
    1. Tennessee--History--Civil War, 1861-1865--Social aspects. 2. United
States--History--Civil War, 1861-1865--Social aspects. 3. Civil-military
relations--Tennessee, Middle--History--19th century. 4. Military occupation--Social
aspects--Tennessee, Middle--History--19th century. 5. Milroy, Robert Huston, 1816-1890.
6. Tennessee--History--Civil War, 1861-1865--Destruction and pillage. 7. United
States--History--Civil War, 1861-1865--Destruction and pillage. 8. Tennessee,
Middle--History, Military--19th century. 9. Tennessee, Middle--Social conditions--19th
19th century. I. Title.

E531 .B73 2003
973.7'09768'5--dc21

                                                                            2002038446

Contents

Illustrations and Maps

Preface

Ideological cleansing. Military and paramilitary units committing mass murder. Bodies left unburied. Ethnic and racial conflict. Prisoners executed without trial. Civilian dwellings destroyed for political purposes. Mass deportations. Civilian informers touching off military raids. Rape. Torture. Looting. Is the scene of these crimes East Timor — 1999? Kosovo — 1998? Bosnia — 1995? Viet Nam — 1973? No, this was Middle Tennessee, 1863–1865. The same scenes were being enacted in all those parts of the South that were under Union military occupation during the years of the Civil War. The story of that occupation is one which historians have never told; indeed, historians have ignored the primary source of official documents which tell the story. In this book will be found a part of the story of that occupation.

In 1996, Milan Hill, a former history teacher at East Middle School in Tullahoma, Tennessee, asked me to involve myself with him and another teacher at that school, Tommy Allen, in working on the records for our area from the provost marshal of the United States Army from the War Between the States era. These two men had discovered the records by sheer curiosity, following leads and assumptions made while investigating local Civil War sites and local history. There are scattered references to provost marshals throughout the *Official Records of the*

War of the Rebellion, and secondary sources occasionally mention the provost of a particular unit, as with General Marsena Patrick, provost marshal of the Army of the Potomac. There is even a small book, *Rebel Watchdog*, by Kenneth Rudley, which deals with the Confederate provost marshal forces. It was clear to Mr. Hill and Mr. Allen that like any other modern army, Civil War-era armies needed a widespread police force, such as the provost marshal, and that records from this force must exist.

We found that the provost marshal dealt with a war within a war. As our investigation proceeded, the three of us learned that some of the duties assigned to the provost marshal during the American Civil War included seeking out and arresting deserters, enemy spies, and civilians suspected of disloyalty; investigating the theft or misuse of government property; controlling travel in the military zone by issuing passes and monitoring government transportation; and maintaining records of persons who gave paroles and who took the Oath of Allegiance. Each army post had a provost marshal who, in addition to carrying out these duties, could also convene courts to try cases involving violations of military orders, departures from the laws of war, and other offenses which arose under military jurisdiction. Since most of Tennessee was a military zone under martial law, the provost marshal handled all manner of disputes that normally would have gone before a civil court. These cases included disputes over property boundaries, ownership of livestock, fair market value of property, fistfights, and breach of the peace. But the provosts also found themselves dealing with rape, arson, robbery, and murder as well as with the military actions of Confederate cavalry units which were dispersed behind Union lines to raid the railroad and the actions of guerrillas and bushwhackers.

In their search for documents about the provost marshal, Mr. Hill and Mr. Allen found two collections of documents totaling four hundred reels of microfilm. The original documents are in the National Archives, but they were fortunate to find copies on microfilm locally. One collection, MC 416, "Union Provost Marshal's Files Relating to Two or more Citizens," was found at Wallace State Community College in Hanceville, Alabama. This collection contains one hundred reels of microfilm which deal with the cases of groups of two or more citizens who became involved with a provost marshal. These documents are arranged both chronologically and alphabetically by the name of the principal civilian involved. This arrangement does not make the collection easy to use, however, since documents relating to different persons who happen to have the same name are often intermingled. Also, there is no geographical order as to the origin of the documents. This means that all documents must be sifted through in order to find those that relate to a particular area.

For several months Mr. Hill and Mr. Allen made a three-hundred-mile round trip on weekends and school holidays to Wallace State Community College, to read the films and make copies of those documents related to the area that included Tullahoma. The town of Tullahoma was the administrative headquarters of an area which the provost marshal records labeled "Military Sub-District #1, Defenses of the Nashville and Chattanooga Railroad." This area included Bedford, Cannon, Coffee, Franklin, Grundy, Lincoln, Marshall, Rutherford, and Warren Counties in Tennessee and Jackson County in Alabama. All of the provost marshals in the subdistrict reported to the commander of the subdistrict who maintained his headquarters at Tullahoma since that town was centrally located along the stretch of track being guarded.

An additional collection of three hundred reels of microfilm, MC 345, "Union Provost Marshal's Files of Papers Relating to Individual Citizens," was located in the Tennessee State Library and Archives in Nashville and was graciously made available to us by interlibrary loan through the library of Motlow State Community College where I am a member of the history faculty. The documents in this collection are arranged alphabetically by the name of the principal civilian involved, and again, documents relating to persons who have the same name are often intermingled. Using this collection was difficult since no chronological or geographical order was observed in the arrangement of the documents.

The lack of organization has made the provost marshal records daunting as a documentary source. Neither a complete index of persons nor any index at all of places exists. All of the provost marshal reports from throughout the United States and the occupied Confederate States are jumbled together without regard to point of origin or, in three-fourths of the reels, to date. Because of this, it is necessary to read the entire four hundred reels of microfilm in order to find the references, if any, to the location or date in which one has an interest. The lack of a complete index of personal names means most names cannot be found without pursuing the same lengthy process.

For example, if Aaron Amos had a horse stolen from him he was the principal person in the case and the provost record is in his name. If one knew such a case existed this record could be easily located. However, Zach Zacharias may have appeared as defendant in the case, but that fact cannot be discerned without reading the case of Aaron Amos. As is evident from this example, the records are not "user-friendly."

As the documents accumulated it became my task to produce a typescript of the material, which proved to be a challenging task. The handwriting varied widely, from beautiful copperplate scripted on good paper with a steel nib pen to a barely legible scrawl scribbled with a blunt pencil on scraps of damp paper. In all cases, spelling was frequently eccentric and punctuation was a matter of personal preference. I have retained the original spelling and punctuation of the documents, except in cases of excessive confusion. The standard for the capitalization of proper nouns differs today, and as such, the original capitalization has been preserved. All inserted grammatical corrections have been set off by square brackets [ ].

Personal names presented a peculiar problem since phonetic spelling was used in taking down testimonies. For example, there are several pages of testimony regarding the "Mopping" family of Bedford County. This testimony was given by recently freed slaves who were still living on the family farm, and was taken down as evidence by clerks in the Provost Marshal's Office at Shelbyville, Tennessee, the county seat of Bedford County. Since the ex-slaves were illiterate, the clerks had to write down what they heard phonetically; the patois of the ex-slaves sounded like "Mopping." Census records reveal that the family name was actually "Maupin."

The records contain a treasure-trove of information about civilian life behind the lines of the occupying army. In the absence of civil law, the provost marshal was responsible for maintaining order and military security, and acted as judge, jury, and executioner in all civilian disputes. The provost records contain a wealth of material that corroborates the contents of the *Official Records* in the matter of guerrilla raids and the activities of irregular troops. Extensive lists of African American army employees exist and material can be gleaned regarding race relations during the war years. The issues of civilian population control and the practice of requiring oaths even to purchase groceries present an entirely different picture of the American Civil War from that often held by both amateur students and many professional historians.

SPECIAL NOTE

A project such as this involves many people. In addition to Mr. Tommy Allen and Mr. Milan Hill, thanks are due to Mrs. Joyce Bateman and the entire circulation staff of the Couch Library at Motlow College, Lynchburg, Tennessee, who helped in securing the microfilm of the provost marshal records and remained cheerful and helpful through many long months. Mr. Gary Davis, genealogist and librarian at Wallace State Community College, Hanceville, Alabama, gave his expertise freely to help with this project. Mr. Chuck Sherrill, formerly with the

Tennessee State Library and Archives was more than generous in making microfilm available. Mr. George Stone, a good friend and compatriot, made a detour while on a personal trip and gave up his time to copy Milroy documents at the Jasper County Indiana Public Library. Without the help of these people, this work could not have been completed and the unknown war revealed in the provost marshal records would have remained unknown, to the detriment of our knowledge of our own history.

Introduction

The popular view of the Civil War is one of armies clashing and flags waving while civilians stand clear of the action. Except for events such as Major General William T. Sherman's "March through Georgia" or Major Generals David Hunter and Philip Sheridan in the Shenandoah Valley, civilians are usually seen as above the fray. The destruction in Georgia and the Shenandoah Valley are looked upon as matters of military necessity, an attack on the enemy infrastructure, similar to a modern bombing campaign. Beyond incidental acts, civilians are not viewed as having been directly affected by the war.

Students with a more sophisticated view of the war know that the plight of the civilians was complex. Civil War armies partially lived off the land; the presence of an army meant the loss of corn, hay, and fodder for livestock even if it did not mean the loss of food stocks for people. Authors, such as Noel Fisher, *War at Every Door*; Daniel Sutherland, *Seasons of War*; Mark Grimsley, *The Hard Hand of War*, and Charles Rice, *Hard Times,* indicate that as the war dragged on, the attitudes of Union authorities changed. Breaking the morale of the Confederate civilian population became an accepted goal of many commanders. But this picture is still incomplete. Life was far more harsh and occupation much more brutal than has been generally conceived. A stark picture of civilian life in the occupied South, and of the attitudes and actions of the Union army, emerges from the records of the provost marshal. These records have been neglected by historians, yet they provide an understanding of the war that is just as important as the one contained in the *Official Records of the War of the Rebellion,* which came into print during the 1880s.

The reports filed by the provost marshal at each military post reveal a civilian society in chaos. Life for civilians behind Union lines tended to be uncertain and unpleasant in most cases. Much of the occupied South was overrun by small units of Confederate guerrillas who damaged Union supply lines and harassed foraging parties. Some of these units were regularly enrolled members of special military units which were permanently dispersed behind Union lines. The members of these units came together at the call of their commander to raid Union positions. John Singleton Mosby in Virginia is perhaps the most celebrated of these guerrilla leaders, but others were to be found throughout the South. Other units, called guerrillas or bushwhackers by the Union authorities, were Confederate Home Guards—overaged men and underaged boys sworn into service to defend their local area and to maintain some degree of order, if not of law. They operated in areas not actually occupied by, but near to, Federal garrisons. Other units were created from civilians seeking revenge against the Yankees, both those "real Yankees" who were from the North and the "Galvanized Yankees," local people who helped the invaders. These individuals, motivated by a desire for revenge, took potshots at isolated opponents as opportunity offered.

All of these acts of opposition caused retaliation by Union forces. Since the guerrillas, who actually committed the acts, were elusive, this retaliation often fell on citizens who were well known, or at least, suspected, to be pro-Confederate. Retaliation often took the form of fines which were used to pay for damaged and lost Union property, seizure of goods, burning houses and farm buildings that might aid guerrillas, and killing both men and women without trial.

These acts of retaliation often were carried out spontaneously by Union authorities, as if these authorities had been taken by surprise by the resistance they faced. In fact, there should have been no surprise at the eruption of irregular warfare in the face of the occupation of Southern territory. The militia system, which had been in place since colonial times, provided a mechanism for calling together an armed force trained in the rudiments of warfare. The Patriot forces had used irregular tactics, including guerrilla raids, against the British in the War of Independence. Spain had given the world the term "guerrilla," or "little war," when the civilians of that nation rose in resistance to the invading French commanded by Napoleon. Lord Wellington, who had been a British participant in the war in Spain against Napoleon, knew how well adapted the American countryside was to such tactics. His respect for the power of guerrilla tactics was one reason he advised the British government to negotiate an end to the War of 1812 instead of attempting to gain a military victory over the United States. The army of the United States had, itself, faced guerrilla opposition during the War with Mexico, especially during Winfield Scott's advance on Mexico City in 1847. These lessons from history had been lost, however, and Union commanders were reduced to inventing responses to irregular warfare.

In an attempt to guide its officers, the United States asked Francis Lieber of Columbia University to develop a code of procedure for dealing with irregular warfare. This code was issued to all Union armies on April 24, 1863, as General Orders #100.[1] These orders said that while the citizens of a hostile country were enemies, and as such, subject to the hardships of war, the principles of civilization dictated that unarmed citizens were to be spared "in person, property, and honor as much as the exigencies of war shall admit." Such citizens were not to be "murdered, enslaved, or carried off to distant parts" while inoffensive citizens were to be disturbed as little as possible.[2] The issue of retaliation was dealt with by saying that while retaliation might be necessary on some occasions its use should be strictly limited and should never be used simply for revenge. Careless use of retaliation, it was stated, "leads nearer to the internecine wars of savages."[3] Private property was protected by the Order and seizure of such property was allowed only in case of crimes or "by way of military necessity." Even in cases of necessity, owners of seized property were to be given receipts for their lost goods.[4] Violence against persons or property was to be punished by death or "such other severe punishment as may seem adequate" while no officer or enlisted man of the United States forces was to be allowed to use his position in a hostile country to make a personal profit by seizing goods.[5] Although the taking of hostages was permitted, the Order stated that "hostages are rare in the present age."[6] Even in the heat of combat, it was "against the usage of modern war to resolve to give no quarter."[7] The practice of showing "no quarter" was banned except in circumstances when a command could not escape entrapment if they were accompanied by prisoners. The knottiest problem was the treatment of soldiers operating behind the lines. The rule laid down in General Orders No. 100 was that members of uniformed units operating behind Union lines were entitled to be treated as prisoners of war, but that those who operated "without commission, and without being part and portion of the organized hostile army" were not prisoners of war but common criminals and should be treated as such.[8] Just what constituted a "uniform" in the tatterdemalion ranks of the Confederacy was subject to debate just as was the "organization" of Confederate units which might, or might not, be part of "the organized hostile army."

The provisions of General Orders No. 100 would be violated on numerous occasions, but since the Order had been issued to all commands, the officers who violated the code could not attempt to excuse themselves by pleading ignorance. The gross nature of many of the violations of the Lieber Code

rose to the level of war crimes. Such crimes brought retaliation by the guerrillas so that, at times, the black flag of revenge
and massacre flew more prominently than either the Stars and
Stripes or the Saint Andrew's cross.

In the southeast corner of Middle Tennessee, along the
line of the Nashville and Chattanooga Railroad, from
Murfreesboro, Tennessee, to Bridgeport, Alabama, life behind
Union lines reached a nadir of human existence. The countryside was stripped of food and of the livestock needed to culti-
vate the fields. Men were largely absent, and the farm economy
was carried on by women and children. Conditions faced by
civilians were as harsh as military law could make them and
the commanders of the district were often as full of spite as
was humanly possible. Union troops occupied Tullahoma and
the surrounding area of Middle Tennessee for several months
during the spring of 1862, following the fall of Nashville and
the Battle of Shiloh and prior to the beginning of the Kentucky
campaign. Scattered provost records exist for that time period,
but in those early days of the war, attitudes had not yet turned
bitter. The Tullahoma campaign of June 24–July 4, 1863,
brought the Union army into Middle Tennessee to stay. Both
the Union and Confederate governments decided to transfer
troops from Virginia to Tennessee in the late summer. The
Confederates arrived in time to participate in, and win, the
battle of Chickamauga. The Union troops arrived too late to
fight in that battle but were used to relieve the siege of Chattanooga and to rescue the Army of the Cumberland. By August
of 1863, General Alpheus Williams, whose division was formerly a part of the Army of the Potomac, was in command of
defending the N&C Railroad and he continued on what he
considered to be dull and thankless duty until the following
spring. Williams was a combat veteran with a good command
record. The defense of Culp's Hill at Gettysburg by troops
under his command had anchored the Union right flank. His
attitude toward the civilian population in his Tennessee zone

of command was one of condescension but not of hatred and oppression.

When Williams was reassigned to combat duty in 1864, Robert H. Milroy was assigned to command the Defenses of the Nashville and Chattanooga Railroad. After Milroy's arrival, the provost marshal records are filled with accounts of civilians suffering for their pro-Confederate views, misdeeds, and crimes, both proven and alleged. Williams had been concerned with protecting the railroad against armed enemies. Milroy was of the opinion that the best way to protect the railroad was to break the will to resist among the population that produced the armed attacks. This policy was much more activist than that of Williams, and would affect the civilian population much more directly. Milroy instituted a program he called "Blood and fire." "Blood and fire is the medicine I use. I shoot the men who are friendly with and harbor bushwhackers and burn their houses."[9]

The Union army was unable to prevent guerrilla activity because their defense of the railroad consisted of blockhouses and small earthwork redoubts placed at bridges, culverts, and water tanks along the rail line. These garrisons were small and their duty was to keep the supply line open, not to occupy the countryside and control the population. Given the geographic area involved, it would not have been possible for the United States to have raised, armed, and supplied a force large enough to garrison every town and village in the South. The garrisons along the railroad were highly susceptible to being overrun, or attacked and pinned down, while the tracks were damaged. The scattering of troops in these semi-isolated garrisons also meant that there was no mass of troops available to chase and disperse guerrilla units. As a result, Union garrisons did not control much of the country beyond the range of the artillery mounted in their fortifications. This was especially the case during the spring of 1864, when the garrisons were composed of third-rate troops not considered fit for combat use.

Beginning in 1864, rear area commanders and their provost marshals had under their command regiments of "100 Day Men," units enlisted for a term of one hundred days and who had minimal training and weak discipline. These men were no match for experienced guerrillas who might be equally, or better, armed than the garrison troops. Such troops were also likely to use harsh, undisciplined methods in dealing with the civilian population that they suspected was helping the guerrillas.

Under Williams and Milroy, dozens of Union officers held the position of provost marshal. Each small garrison had someone detailed to this rotating duty. Thus, over the years, numerous men reported to the General Commanding Military Sub-District #1 of Middle Tennessee, Defenses of the N&C Railroad, even though some of these men served as provost marshal for only a few days or weeks. For reasons best known to the military bureaucracy of that day, their reports and the orders of the general commanding are today part of the provost marshal records.

The Confederates in the Middle Tennessee area generally operated under the Partisan Ranger Act of April 1863, by which the Confederate Congress had authorized military operations behind enemy lines and had allowed for the organization of regularly enrolled forces to carry out such operations. Around the Tullahoma area leaders such as George Hays, Robert Blackwell, Milus Johnson, Lemuel Mead, Frank Gurley, and Champ Ferguson were found. The cavalry command of General Nathan Bedford Forrest, persistent raider of Union supply lines, always lurked in the wings. Forrest was stationed in Northern Mississippi and made life miserable for Union commanders sent against him. He was so efficient in destroying Union advances and disrupting their rear areas that in the summer of 1864 General Joseph Johnston, who commanded the Army of Tennessee against the army group led by General William Sherman, advocated abandoning Mississippi to allow

Forrest to wreak havoc against the N&C Railroad. Forrest made one foray into the area upon which the guerrillas and partisans flocked to join him in an unsuccessful attempt against the main Union supply line. That these guerrillas were a deadly annoyance is testified to by Milroy who said, "murder by bushwhackers is a daily occurrence among us."

Guerrilla leaders did not write "after-combat" reports detailing their actions. If the Partisan Cavalry in Tennessee did file such records, they are lost. No collection of letters from any of these guerrilla fighters has surfaced, and none of their leaders had the charisma to attract biographers, as has been the case with the better known Mosby in Virginia. Therefore, most of what is known of these Confederates has come from the lips of their enemies, a less than reliable source.

Even when it proved impossible to exterminate all of the guerrillas, Union commanders attempted to destroy their base of support within the community by encouraging informers among the pro-Union elements of the population. In one case, 75 names appear on a list of "disloyal" persons turned in by Moses Pittman. Action was taken against those on this list based on no other evidence than the accusation of one man. An examination of the 1860 census reveals that Pittman was a distiller and that many of the individuals he accused were business competitors.

Little value was placed on human life in Middle Tennessee under a provost marshal who was willing to kill citizens on the basis of mere suspicion. As Robert Milroy put it, "I have fell on a plan to stir up the people against the monsters [the guerrillas] and to pitch in and help us clean the country out. Blood and fire is the medicine I use. I shoot the men who are friendly with and harbor bushwhackers and burn their houses. By spreading death and fire in a neighborhood where the bushwhackers have a friend, the survivors come rushing in demanding in terror 'What must we do to be saved?' I tell them to organize companies — get guns, horse clubs, or anything else —

and rush out after the bushwhackers — kill or capture them and bring them in and we will be their friends and protect them."[10]

Milroy found gleeful supporters for his policy of blood and fire among his subordinates. General Eleazer A. Paine was one such supporter who "had about two hundred guerrillas shot since he has been stationed here. It is not often that his men bring in any that they capture, when they do, and Paine ascertains them to be guerrillas beyond a doubt he orders them quietly walked outside the pickets and shot and no report is made of the matter and nothing is said about it. Two of them have been shot that way since I come here. I would not have known anything of it had I not happened on their dead bodies in riding out."[11]

With such staunch supporters as Paine, is it any wonder that for those who supported the Confederacy, Milroy's tenure in command became a reign of terror? The records of the provost marshal illustrate a side of the war that varies immensely from the usual battles, campaigns, and marches. For civilians living behind the lines, the war was a story of murder, robbery, and betrayal. It was truly an experience from which they never recovered but at best endured.

1

The Unknown Battlefield

In February 1862, the Union armies in the West began to put into operation the "Anaconda Strategy" suggested by General Winfield Scott. This broadly conceived plan emphasized the use of two major Union advantages: the possession of a navy and an industrial base which would make possible the building of an even larger navy. The existing "blue water" navy would be used to blockade the Confederate ports, shutting off the flow of badly needed manufactured materials from Europe and preventing Confederate cotton from going to Europe to become the basis of payment for military goods. The newly constructed "brown water" navy would be used to gain control of the many navigable rivers which penetrated Confederate territory and would then use army troops to subdue and to occupy the areas.

Beginning in February 1862, at Fort Henry and Fort Donelson in Tennessee, the Anaconda Strategy led to the occupation of the state capital of Nashville and the major city of Memphis on the Mississippi. In the spring of 1862, the Union navy captured New Orleans, closing the mouth of the Mississippi, and in July 1863, a combined army and navy expedition took Vicksburg. With the surrender of Vicksburg all of the Mississippi River had come under Union control. In 18 months the Anaconda Strategy had brought much of the western area

of the Confederacy under Union control. Confederate coun-
terattacks at Shiloh and the Kentucky campaign during the
autumn of 1862 slowed and limited the success of the Union
plan, but the pattern of success was clear.

By early January 1863, following the bloody fighting at
Murfreesboro on the banks of the Stones River, the major Union
force in Tennessee, the Army of the Cumberland, needed to
make a new departure. There were no rivers for the army to
utilize in its advance toward the rail junction town of Chattanooga. Although Chattanooga is on the Tennessee River, the
river's course is circuitous and navigation is hampered by
Mussel Shoals in the northwest corner of Alabama. Because of
this, the river could not be used as a supply route. In order to
reach Chattanooga, the Army of the Cumberland would have
to modify the Anaconda Strategy and substitute a railroad for
a river.

The Nashville and Chattanooga Railroad (N&C) was the
route the Union army chose. The railroad began in Nashville
and crossed the fertile Cumberland Basin of Middle Tennessee, climbed to the Highland Rim in an area known as the "Oak
Barrens," and then penetrated the rugged terrain of the
Cumberland Plateau before joining the tracks of the Memphis
and Charleston Railroad (M&C) at Stevenson, Alabama. From
that point, the N&C and the M&C used the same tracks to reach
Chattanooga, crossing the Tennessee River at Bridgeport, Alabama. Perhaps the most striking feature of the road was a 2,200-
foot-long tunnel which passed through Sewanee Mountain
near Cowan, Tennessee. The Army of the Cumberland would
follow this band of rails in carrying out the Anaconda Strategy. Of course, the Confederate Army of Tennessee would use
the same rail line in an attempt to frustrate the Union plans.

The N&C was the only feasible line of advance and the
only direct line of supply for Union forces moving farther
south. The line of the Decatur and Nashville Railroad (D&N)
ran from Nashville to Decatur, Alabama, and near there joined

the M&C, but that route to Chattanooga was longer and much more exposed to interruption by Confederate forces. Because of this, the Army of Tennessee would attempt to hold the N&C; if it were lost, the rails would become a logical target for Rebel cavalry and irregular forces.

General William S. Rosecrans took six months to prepare the Army of the Cumberland for its forward movement along the N&C. From January to June 1863, he rearmed his cavalry, gathered supplies, and collected reinforcements. On June 24, 1863, Rosecrans struck at the right flank of the Army of Tennessee commanded by Braxton Bragg. In a brilliant campaign of maneuver lasting 11 days, Rosecrans forced Bragg from his position along the Duck River and sent the Confederates in retreat to Chattanooga.[1] Even there, Bragg did not feel safe, and he abandoned the town with only the barest gesture at defense.

Bragg could have held Chattanooga for a considerably longer period had he chosen to because the N&C was not in condition to handle supplies. The Union Pioneer Brigade under Brigadier General James St. Clair Morton had repaired the line from Murfreesboro, Rosecrans' original base, to Stevenson, Alabama, with amazing speed. Only a few miles farther toward Chattanooga, the retreating Rebels had destroyed the rail bridge over the Tennessee River at Bridgeport. Replacing this major span would require some time.

While the combat soldiers settled into camp for a few days of rest, those men assigned to the provost marshal were already performing a routine duty: collecting and forwarding prisoners. On July 14, 10 days after arriving at the top of the Cumberland Plateau, Luther P. Bradley's brigade reported that it was still receiving prisoners. From the campus of the University of the South, Bradley's provost marshal reported 27 prisoners and refugees. Among those listed were G. J. Simons, William Higgerson, J. A. Hensley, Noy Holden, William Richardson, L. V. Hensley, and T. V. Adams.[2] These men all belonged to the 23rd and 24th Tennessee Infantry regiments, units which had been recruited in the Middle Tennessee area. It appears that when their homes came under Union occupation, these men felt a strong urge to return to protect their families and property. Although they are listed as "prisoners of war," there had been no combat in which they had been captured, so it is reasonable to believe that they surrendered in an attempt to go home. There would be other men who would avoid the net of the provost marshal. They would return to their homes and, in many cases, become recruits for the guerrilla bands which caused the Union provost marshal so much trouble over the next two years.

At the same time, those who could prove their loyalty to the Union were being rewarded by having their property protected. On July 18, 1863, the Union authorities in Manchester, the county seat of Coffee County, Tennessee, published a list of names of citizens who had been granted "protection papers." The list included

A. J. Christian	James Winton	Jesse Wooton
William Winton	James Lusk	Wm Ray
John D. Berry	James G. Parsefell — All of Grundy County	
Joel Hale	W. J. Lindley — both of Coffee County[3]	

Some of these individuals were from families with male relatives in Confederate service. Already the foundation was being laid for social conflict and disruption.

Meanwhile, the guerrillas were gathering. On July 7 Rosecrans sent a circular to his corps commanders, Generals Thomas Crittenden, George Thomas, and Alexander McCook, which indicated that straggling soldiers had been committing outrages on citizens by robbing and thieving and quartermasters were taking forage improperly. Rosecrans ordered his corps commanders to crack down on such practices. At the same time, General Philip H. Sheridan was told to control his troops and to enforce proper discipline. Rosecrans noted, "Disloyalty does not forfeit the rights of humanity which every true soldier will respect." Chief of Staff James A. Garfield noted, "The lawlessness of our soldiers on foraging parties will make bushwhackers faster than any other thing."[4] These words proved to be prophetic.

Opposition to the Union presence began atop the Cumberland Plateau at Tracy City in Grundy County, the very area where most of those granted "protection" at Manchester had come from. The soldiers involved came from Luther P. Bradley's brigade.

> Head Qrs 3 Brigade 3 Div
> 20 Army Corps July 24, 1863

Captain

> I send in this morning a man by the name of "Myers" whom I arrested at Tracy City yesterday. He is said by the Henleys and other Union men to be a thoroughly bad fellow and is charged with part of the late outrages at Tracy City. Mr Best and Dr Reebe who go to Cowan this morning will furnish the Provost Marshal with some facts which will warrant the detention.

> I can get a quantity of potatoes at Tracy City by sending out for them if the Quarter Mast is authorized to pay for them out of funds in his hands, at the rate of 11.00 per bush. I would like to know if such a purchase will be strictly proper. I can get several hundred bushels in that neighborhood if they are wanted by the Division. They can be taken and receipted for, of course. But the owners are loyal men I believe. And POOR!

> Respectfully
> L.P. Bradley, Col Comdg

Capt Geo Lee, Adj 3 Div[5]

Myers soon found himself in serious trouble as the army high command became involved. Rosecrans ordered his acting provost marshal general, Captain R. M. Goodwin, to order Captain G. S. Ranson, provost of Bradley's brigade, to forward all evidence against Myers to Department Headquarters since he was suspected of being a bushwhacker.[6]

The language used in the case of Myers represents one of the problems of working with the provost marshal records. The term "bushwhacker" was in general use, but no legal definition was ever given to the term, nor is "guerrilla" ever defined. Apparently, anyone who took a shot at Union forces from cover and who was acting alone was labeled a "bushwhacker," while a guerrilla acted in concert with others. On some occasions, however, Confederate cavalry forces on a raid against Union communications were called "guerrillas." The other problem represented by the Myers case is that the rest of the story is missing. The records do not indicate what happened to Myers. Later in the war there would be good reason to suspect that he simply would have been taken out and shot.

Although Myers may have acted alone, evidence exists that bands of guerrillas were operating in the area. First Lieutenant C. Montague, serving as provost marshal, sent a list of four prisoners of war to Army Headquarters. Three were identified as belonging to various Confederate regiments but the fourth was John Short. Beside his name is the note, "Short is said to belong to Gunters band of Murders and Robbers that infest these mountains."[7] Gunter was a prominent landowner in North Alabama whose holdings included the current town of Guntersville. Short was the name of a prominent family in Middle Tennessee whose lands reached into Alabama. Short was captured at Sewanee, Tennessee, just a few miles from the area known as Short Springs.

Soon there would be more cases, these leading to Union deaths. On August 3, 1863, just north of the village of Hillsboro, and not far from the line of the N&C, Private Abner Tull, Company D, 13th Michigan Infantry, was shot by a local citizen, John W. Johnson. A few days later, Johnson was arrested and sent to Murfreesboro where he was tried by a military commission. Found guilty of murder, he was sent to Nashville and there was hanged at the state penitentiary. A month later, near the same location, Private William A. Bault, Company A, 3rd Kentucky Infantry, was killed by a civilian, Alexander P. Anderson. As a result, Anderson was sentenced to five years in the state penitentiary.[8] The numbers and military effect of these guerrillas would increase until the end of the war and would provide a major focus of the work of the provost marshals. The military significance of the N&C, and the need to protect the vital rails, would produce a bitter struggle in Middle Tennessee.

The battle of Chickamauga temporarily changed the strategic situation in Middle Tennessee. The defeat and entrapment of the Army of the Cumberland at Chattanooga not only placed the strategic initiative in the hands of the Confederates, it placed even greater focus on the N&C. It was imperative to keep the rails open as far toward Chattanooga as possible. A rugged mountain track led in a roundabout fashion almost 60 miles from Stevenson to Chattanooga. Only a trickle of supplies flowed along that route and if the rails were cut between Stevenson and Nashville, the problem of supply would become insoluble. Further, the Army of the Potomac was rushing the army corps commanded by Generals Henry W. Slocum and Joseph Hooker to reinforce Ulysses S. Grant so that Grant could relieve the Yanks trapped at Chattanooga. Sabotage or destruction of the railroad would inhibit this rescue attempt. Part of Slocum's XII Corps was a division commanded by General Alpheus Williams. Williams found his division blocked at Nashville because a guerrilla raid had destroyed the tracks south of there. It took Williams from October 5 to October 12 to move by rail from Nashville to Decherd, a distance of less than one hundred miles.[9] In short, he could have marched the distance in less time. Already the guerrillas were proving a hindrance to the Union war effort. After having traveled by rail all the way from Louisville, Kentucky, to Decherd, Williams noted, "This is a monstrous line over which General

Rosecrans has to supply his army, over 300 miles of railroad, crossed every few miles by broad streams and valleys and running through and around and across high mountains. I can't see how the Army can be supplied at Chattanooga unless the Rebs are driven off and the railroad opened its whole length. Even then, it will be a most insecure line, liable to constant interruption, and of a length that forbids protection."[10] Clearly, protecting the N&C was crucial to Union success.

Civilians who lived along the route of advance began to feel the heavy hand of war on their shoulders, as food and forage were swept up by the Union forces. The troops involved in gathering supplies showed no respect for political opinions or for the documents that many civilians believed offered protection from seizure for their property. The Union supply route to Chattanooga ran through the Sequatchie Valley, and the fate of a pro-Union family there illustrates the way in which war spared no one.

Jasper Oct 13th 1863

Lt Col Wiles
Provost Marshall General
Sir

I regret the circumstances should render it necessary for me to report the following facts. On the 13th ins Lieut Wm. I. Borland of the 10th Ohio Cavalry being then in charge of a Forage Train came to the house of I.G. Kelly one of the truly loyal men of the country and in violation of a Safeguard given him by Gen Rosecrans loaded (5) five wagons with corn intended for the use of the family of Mr Kelly saying that "Damn the Safeguard, I will take the corn any how" or words to that effect. Mr Kelly has rendered valuable services to Gen Rosecrans and the Gen wishing to protect his property so much at least as his family should require, gave him the safeguard. The facts being reported to me by Mr Kelly I stopped the wagons containing the corn when they arrived here and should have returned them with the corn to the owner but shortly afterwards received a preemptor order from Gen Morgan to permit the wagons to go with the corn to Battle Creek. Mr Kelly lives about 3 1/2 miles north of Jasper. I have endeavored to prevent excesses in foraging in this vicinity but find it a very difficult matter to do so.

> Very Respectfully, your Obdt Servant
> W.F. Prosper
> Major comdg Post Jasper Tenn[11]

The reply from Lieutenant William Borland arrived at the provost marshal in short order. The lieutenant felt his actions were justified, and the provost agreed.

In compliance with orders from Head Quarters I left Battle Creek Tenn on the morning of the 13th ins in charge of a Forage Train of eighteen wagons my instructions were to proceed beyond Jasper Tenn and load with corn four (4) miles northeast of Jasper I found sufficient in a field to load seven (7) wagons. After scouting the country and failing to find any more corn either in the fields or elsewhere I started on my return to camp when within about three (3) miles from Jasper I found a crib of corn belonging to a Mr Kelly as I understand. Mr. Kelly was not at home but his wife informed me that he had "Protection Papers" which she could not produce as Mr Kelly had them with him. Knowing that forage was not usually exempt in such cases I proceeded to load five (5) wagons leaving what I supposed to be about twenty five (25) bushels of ear for the use of Mr Kelly family consisting of four (4) persons in all. When the wagons were nearly loaded Mr K returned and showed me a document signed by Gen Rosecrans protecting his "personal property." I treated this paper and Mr Kelly with all due respect using no improper language in reference to either, but in view of the facts determined to report to Gen Morgan with the corn which I knew was much needed. Having still six empty wagons I

had proceeded as far as Jasper when an officer represent-
ing himself as Commander of the post stopped the said
five wagons and ordered me to return with the corn to Mr
Kelly's this I declined to do until I had reported the trans-
action to Gen Morgan at Battle Creek in person, who gave
me a written order for the Officer in Command at Jasper
to release the corn, which he did, and I reported with it at
Battle Creek without further trouble.

> Very Respect. Your Obdt Servant
> W.D. Borland
> 2d Lieut Co D 10th OVC[12]

This single action would reduce the Kelly family to pov-
erty. The family would have no animals surviving the winter
to make a crop and there would be insufficient food to feed
the family during the winter. It might be noted that 25 bushels
of corn still on the cob would produce only a fraction of that
number of bushels once the corn was shelled. This means the
Kelly family did not have enough corn for meal for the months
until the next crop would mature, even if they had enough
corn left for seed to plant another crop. Certainly there would
have been no corn to feed mules or cows during the winter.
The Kellys, note, were described as "Loyal"; if this were the
fate of those who were pro-Union, what would life under Union
occupation be like for those who supported the Confederacy?
Lieutenant Borland had stated the priorities quite clearly when
he said the corn was "much needed." The needs and wants of
the Union army would come above all else.

After the battles around Chattanooga in November 1863,
the N&C became even more important. The Union army was
now an additional 130 miles away from its major supply depot at Nashville. A base of supplies had to be built up in order
to protect the Northern hold on Chattanooga and to prepare
for any move into north Georgia. Although the Decatur and
Nashville (D&N, sometimes called the Tennessee and Alabama,
or T&A, in some reports from 1864) would provide subsidiary

help, and even though limited supplies could reach Chattanooga via the Tennessee River, the N&C would be the major supply line for the primary Union effort in the West in 1864.

By mid-December the Pioneer Brigade had the rail line open and supplies began to flow into Chattanooga in increasing amounts.[13] Every day 10 trains, consisting of 10 cars each, left Nashville to make the trip across Middle Tennessee, through the Cumberlands, and over the Tennessee River, to the Union forces at Chattanooga.

General Sherman thought it was dangerous to risk his armies at the end of a lengthy supply line. As the plans for the Overland Campaign of 1864 began to develop, Sherman determined that he would not risk his armies at the far end of such a tenuous lifeline as the Louisville and Nashville (L&N) and the N&C; especially since his movement south into Georgia would make him dependent on the Western and Atlantic (W&A), which connected Chattanooga with Atlanta. To prevent his army from being cut off from supplies by guerrillas and raiders, Sherman determined to build up a depot of materials sufficient to support his army for several days in Chattanooga. Even if the N&C were cut, food and ammunition could continue to flow down the W&A. Confederate strategy would either be to wreck the W&A close behind Sherman's front lines, a difficult task because of the presence of so many Union troops, or to destroy the N&C so thoroughly that the depot at Chattanooga would be depleted and a Union retreat would be mandated by a lack of supplies.[14]

The Confederate government was well aware of the military opportunities offered by Sherman's lengthy rail supply line, and they were equally aware of the difficulties involved with exploiting these opportunities. Guerrillas would become very active in attempting to wreck the rail line, and Union countermeasures would reflect the importance placed on keeping the line open.

General Nathan Bedford Forrest represented the best hope the Confederates had that Sherman's supply lines could be cut

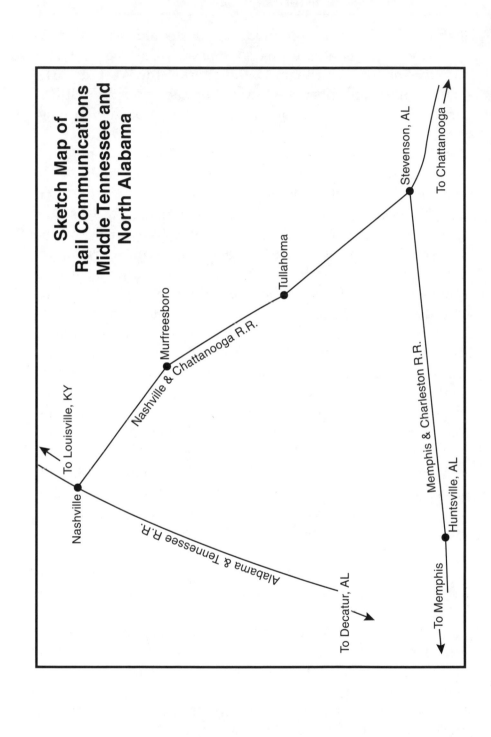

Sketch Map of
Rail Communications
Middle Tennessee and
North Alabama

To Louisville, KY

Nashville

Alabama & Tennessee R.R.

To Decatur, AL

Murfreesboro

Nashville & Chattanooga R.R.

Tullahoma

Stevenson, AL

To Chattanooga

Memphis & Charleston R.R.

Huntsville, AL

To Memphis

and the Yankees left to starve in Georgia. By this point in the war Forrest was a leader of legendary proportions. On September 19 Forrest united his command with that of Philip Roddy at Cherokee, Alabama, and crossed the Tennessee River the next day. With about 4,500 men Forrest reached Athens, Alabama, on the T&A Railroad and captured the Federal garrison of the town on September 24. The following day Forrest captured the garrison that protected the Sulpher Creek trestle on the T&A, and burned the three-hundred-foot-long bridge. After making a feint on Pulaski, a town too heavily fortified and garrisoned for Forrest to attack, the cavalryman moved east toward Tullahoma and the N&C. The Duck River bridge at Normandy and the tunnel at Cowan were the most vulnerable parts of the road in the Tullahoma area.

By this time Sherman was growing concerned about his supply lines even though Atlanta had been captured in early September. In order to protect his supply line to the fallen citadel, Sherman ordered troops be sent from Georgia, Kentucky, Indiana, Ohio, and West Tennessee to hem in Forrest and destroy him. Well aware of the odds growing against him, and of the strength of the Union defenses on the railroad, Forrest withdrew by way of Huntsville.[15] This reaction on the part of Sherman and his subordinates illustrates quite clearly the strategic importance of the corridor through which the N&C passed and highlights the significance of the provost marshal records for the area.

Before and after the main armies began their movements, the N&C corridor served as a conduit for spies, smugglers, and those hardy souls who carried mail back and forth between Confederate- and Union-occupied territories. Even as his Army of the Cumberland lay at Murfreesboro, Rosecrans was seeking and receiving information about what lay to his south along the railroad. John O. Nobel, chief of scouts for the army, sent out S. N. Graves to travel through Huntsville and Bridgeport to contact local residents who were thought to be friendly to the Union cause. Graves successfully completed his mission and reported making contact with an old man named "Hendricks who lives three miles beyond Versailles, is a Justice of the Peace & a sound Union man, a man of more than ordinary intelligence."[16] Hendricks was to be a link in a chain of civilian informers and collectors of information which Rosecrans would establish all the way from Murfreesboro to Chattanooga. Some of the information was volunteered by citizens passing through the Union lines, either on business or as refugees moving north to get away from the war. Typical of these reports is that of T. S. Williamson of Bedford County who came into Union lines on February 15, 1863. He reported that "I left home this morning about daylight. Wheeler, Forrest & Starnes are now at Columbia. Wheeler left Shelbyville last Monday. The three divisions still at Shelbyville, this I know to be true. Jarrets Gin House and ten bales of cotton was burned last night. Also Dr Hoggarts with fifty bales of cotton. Jarrets was burned by men dressed in Federal uniforms. Six guerrillas passed my house yesterday evening. They are scouting from Middleton to Eagleville. My son went to Chapel Hill yesterday. Roddeys Regt is at that place. Last night in the burning of Dr Hoggarts gin they tried to capture his Negroes. Sixty of them ran away and came into our lines."[17] The reports of the strength and location of Confederate troops were useful to Rosecrans but so were the reports about burning cotton. The Confederates would not be destroying this valuable commodity unless they felt it was likely to fall into Union hands.

Another report arrived six weeks later, which, like the previous civilian report, was amazingly accurate in describing the positions of Confederate army units.

Triune April 30 1863

Statement of a Union Refugee

My name is Henry C. Hall—am twenty two years of age—live five miles east of Lewisburg, Marshall Co Tenn. Was conscripted in January last, escaped and have been lying in the woods most of the time since—Tried to escape into West Tenn, started April 20th, went as far as Lynville and was turned back, started for Nashville April 24th, crossed Duck River four miles above Chapel Hill, came to Henry Black's near Eagleville and stayed there until last evening, came to the picket below Triune this morning.

It was currently reported that Forrest with his command went to Florence about the 26th of April, that Bragg's main force was removed from Tullahoma to Wartrace or Shelbyville about April 23rd, am certain that one division went from Tullahoma to Wartrace about that time. It was reported that Bragg has been reinforced by Buckner with about 20,000 men. Do not believe that the number was really so large as reported.

Patterson is at Chapel Hill with about four hundred cavalry. Russel at Unionville with four or five hundred. Van Dorn was about Spring Hill with his main force.

Large numbers are deserting from Braggs army, particularly men from Alabama and Miss. Bragg keeps a stronger guard in his rear than in his front. Soldiers live on half rations or less of bacon and corn meal. Can get no beef since the Federals have invested the lines at Vicksburg and Port Hudson.

Citizens are getting alarmed about subsistence for their families. Gold sells at 550 and state money from 200 to 300 per cent.

Want to take the Oath of Allegiance and go North.

Hall appears intelligent and honest in his professions and statements.

J.M. Schofield
Brig Genl[18]

Just a month before beginning the Tullahoma campaign, Rosecrans received a report that was several months old but still contained valuable information about the conditions on the N&C.

Statement of Wm Harwell

On the 13th of Oct [1862] I left Loudon and traveled along the RR via Chattanooga to Wartrace the road in many places was nearly impassable cars in a very worn condition & the conductor frequently ordered the passengers from one car to another. Rolling stock is very scarce on the road. Broken cars were laying nearly all along the road.

As I returned on the 25th they were very busily engaged in repairing.

In passing through the tunnel [at Cowan] the cars tilted so much as to strike the sides with force enough to shatter the windows and shivver the top railing. I have lived for some time on or near the RR & say that in ordinary times no sane man would attempt to run the RR in the condition it is in & hands are not in the country to keep it up or put it in reasonable repair.

There were no fortifications around Chattanooga, saw a rifle pit dug on the 25th of October.

Murfreesboro May 23 1863 Wm. M. R. Howell

This man doubtlessly tells the truth. The plan spoken of would be attempted if support was known to be anywhere near when the attempt was made. ── says several were hung and shot because the effort was premature. All they want to know is that we will be with them in a reasonable time.

Hale

I find upon inquiring that the tunnel on the Ga road and Cleveland road are walled and arched with brick.

Jas T. Shelley
Col 5th Regt East Tenn Vols[19]

The "plan" spoken of by Hale was a plan to sabotage the railroad by burning bridges and blocking tunnels to disrupt Confederate supplies and reinforcements once the Army of the

Cumberland moved forward. There had been a similar plan in 1862 during the first Union incursion into Middle Tennessee, but that plan failed because the Union army did not press deeply enough into Confederate territory. The result of the timidity with which the army advanced was the execution of several Unionist civilians in the area around Knoxville. Unwilling to risk such retaliation, Howell wanted reassurance that this time the Union army would really come to the aid of the saboteurs.

Of course, not all the spies were pro-Union. The Confederacy also had formal and informal sources of information flowing through the N&C corridor. Those spies who were unfortunate enough to be caught appear in the records of the provost marshal. One of these was a man named Rose who was questioned by Captain A. B. Carroll of the Provost Marshal's Office. Based on what he learned from the interrogation, Captain Carroll charged Rose with carrying letters through Union lines to Confederate soldiers. One letter addressed to Colonel Ester of the Confederate army had been found in Rose's possession. Rose had been captured by a deception. Carroll had sent a man in a butternut uniform to Rose's house "to play off Rebel on him." Rose had been taken in by the fake rebel and told all he knew about Union plans and had passed on the letter for delivery.[20]

The use of disguises and double agents would become commonplace as the war continued. Rose and his fellow prisoners were the forerunners of many people who would find themselves on the way to prison because they were accused of helping bushwhackers or who had been gullible enough to be taken in by double agents such as the "man disguised in a butternut suit" who was sent to Rose's house to "play off Rebel on him."

Some of the Confederate spies were more successful in penetrating Union lines, if not any more successful than Rose had been in exiting them. In January 1863, J. T. Fletcher was arrested by Union army police on charges of attempting to go through the army lines without a pass. Letters to persons behind Confederate lines were found on his person as well as other incriminating evidence of spying. Fletcher had come to Nashville from Chattanooga with other refugees and "contrabands," that is, escaped slaves. Claiming to be a Union supporter, Fletcher said he was travelling to his parents' home to stay with them. Since Nashville had a population of about five thousand at that time, it was relatively easy for the police to keep an eye on the erstwhile "refugee." Within a week police heard a rumor that Fletcher was going to "run the lines." Upon his arrest, Fletcher was ready to leave Nashville and admitted that he was a Confederate sympathizer. "It is respectfully submitted," wrote the provost to Army Headquarters, "that he is a dangerous person to remain here in these lines that there is no proper place to secure him here, that there is no proper tribunal for his trial, that therefore he be committed to the Military prison at Alton in the state of Illinois for trial." This suggestion was approved and General Rosecrans ordered that J. T. Fletcher "be confined in the Alton Illinois Military Prison during the present war or until tried unless he should be released by the commanding general of the Department."[21]

It should be noted that Rosecrans, a military officer, took the authority to order a civilian imprisoned without trial for the duration of the war or at the pleasure of the department commander. Information was too precious to allow the Confederates untrammeled use of the N&C corridor.

Considering the number of letters seized, there must have been a very large volume of mail crossing the lines. Much of the mail was purely of a personal nature, but still reveals significant details about life on both sides of the battlefront. The army commanders were anxious to stop all such communications. On December 12, 1862, General George W. N. Nelson, commanding Union forces at Gallatin, Tennessee, intercepted a letter from Dr. Jesse A. Blackmore, who was with the

Confederate army at Shelbyville, Tennessee, to his wife at
Gallatin. The letter was being carried by a "Negro servant of
Dr. Blackmore." General Nelson reported his intention of dis-
guising one of his men in butternut clothing and delivering
the letter to Mrs. Blackmore. It was rumored that she served
as an unofficial postmistress, collecting letters for Confederate soldiers and sending them to her husband for delivery as
often as once a week. The couriers who were used to carry the
mail back and forth across Union lines were slaves of the
Blackmore family. The doctor said:

> My dear Wife,
>
> It is now one month since I left home and this is the
> third time I have written to you and have not recd any-
> thing from you. You must have got my letters sent from
> Cairo by Cunningham, as Dr Thomas wrote to Morgan
> by him. I think you might have written by him, and have
> sent me a shirt or two, as you know I have none but the
> one on me. I now beg you to send me two or three shirts,
> my undershirt and drawers, a pair or two of socks, a black
> cravat and pocket handkerchief. I am very much in need
> of a coat and waistcoat, do send me enough cloth to make
> them, send the piece of check-a-linsey I bought and do-
> mestic enough for pockets and lining, thread and buttons,
> if to be got, for there is nothing of the kind here. If the
> things I ask you for could be bought here I would not
> trouble you. I wish you to send jeans enough to make G.
> an overcoat the same you made for the negroes will do
> very well. How are you getting along with the Abolition-
> ists, have they treated you with any indignity, and what
> are they doing with the property? Are they taking any
> stock or corn, wheat, or hay? I send you two hundred
> dollars in money and R.A. Bennett's check on Joel
> Tumpkins for one hundred dollars, one hundred for your
> own use, and I want one hundred dollars given to Hebb
> Allen for the use of Margaret Allen, take his receipt for it,

the check give to Fooshee, tell him to collect it for his own use. Tell him to have the stock well fed particularly the brood mare, and the sows & pigs if the Yankees have left anything to feed with.

I was at Shelbyville last week, and much gratified to see our soldiers pretty well provided with clothes, blankets, & etc and much delighted to see them in such high spirits, and eager for the fight (they will fight to the death) particularly the Tenn boys. Buckner's division moved from Shelbyville for Fredonia Friday and Saturday other divisions are moving towards Nashville, the object seems to be to drive the enemy inside their fortifications. Joseph E. Johnston is here and will act in concert with Bragg, his arrival has had a most cheering effect with the army and country, and there is now strong hopes we will be able to hold middle Tenn. I saw yesterday between 1500 and 2000 Yankees at Blacks Cross Roads taken by Morgan at Hartsville on Sunday morning. He got their entire force there, I look upon it as one of the most daring feats known in the annals of warfare, taking the character of the weather, the position of the enemy on the north of a river, and so close a position to large reinforcements. Morgan has been in the bed since his return from the expedition from Pneumonia brought on by the bad weather and exposure. I talked with him yesterday, he thought he would be up today. Tell my brother in law, Colonel G, from what I hear from him he is too despondent, say to him to cheer up, that our cause must triumph. It is said President Davis has issued a proclamation to retaliate on Lincoln's emancipation policy by putting a Yankee prisoner to work under a negro overseer for every negro taken from his owner.

If Thompkins pays Fooshee the check in Confederate money send it to me. You had best send me all the confederate money you have got, as you cannot use it there. I would like to have Bockus and Matt here as they are doing nothing there. I have learned they would not come when I sent for them fearing I would sell them, assure them I have no intention if they behave themselves, whether they come or not. Buy and send the young black man as the Yankees will take him. Your mother is much better now, she is very weak but not suffering much, my presence has seemed to be a great consolation to her. G will remove on this side of the river and will bring this letter to you, and after remaining a day or two with his family across the river & return here with G. Do send the articles I have mentioned as I can get nothing here.

If you see any of Colonel P's family say to them that Brother L got over safe, and met Major P at Blacks Crossroads and went to Fredonia with him, where his command is camped. I saw your brother there, his wife and friend some days since, they are all well, the Dr's wife seems to be a very pleasant lady. I think I will try and get [illegible] here out of the federal lines, as he may be forced off by them, and as his wife is in Nashville he may go with them voluntarily. I heard of his trying to get Major G the owner of his wife to get him a pass to go and see her.

Yours Affectionately

B

P.S. write and give me all the news.[22]

This letter not only contains accurate information about Confederate troop movements prior to the battle of Stones River, it also reveals a great deal by implication about race relations. Although the Emancipation Proclamation was about to become effective, Tennessee was exempt from its provisions. The Army of the Cumberland, made up largely of Midwesterners, was not enthusiastic about emancipation at any rate, and never did have the reputation of actively trying to separate slaves from their owners unless the owners were known Confederates. Dr. and Mrs. Blackmore entrusted not only letters but also large sums of cash to the care of one of their slaves who regularly traveled between Union and Confederate territory.

Some mail carriers were merely soldiers going home on furlough who offered to carry letters to "the folks back home." Such was a risky business if "home" was behind Union lines because carrying letters laid the carrier open to charges of spying instead of being treated as an ordinary prisoner of war. John Hudson of Gallatin County, Kentucky, provides one example. Hudson was stationed with the Confederate cavalry under General Joseph Wheeler guarding the right flank of the Southern line. Although stationed at the village of Beech Grove where he helped guard the vital Murfreesboro Road as it passed through Hoovers Gap, Hudson got a furlough to go home. To help pay for his expenses Hudson agreed to carry mail to soldiers' families back in Kentucky. The recipients were to give Hudson five dollars in exchange for delivery of the letters. For an additional fee Hudson agreed to carry letters back to the Confederacy. The provost records indicate that one of Hudson's fellow soldiers deserted and, on arriving in Kentucky, informed Federal authorities that Hudson was in the area and that he was carrying mail from Confederate soldiers. Hudson was arrested and sent to Camp Chase where along with Robert White he was to stand a court-martial for "delivering letters across enemy lines."[23] Five dollars, each way, was a considerable monetary compensation for carrying letters, but obviously, the risk was also high. If the "folks at home" wanted to hear from the "boys at the front" they were equally anxious to write to them and ran high risks themselves.

William Truesdale was chief of army police for the Army of the Cumberland and was especially zealous in stopping communications across the lines. His zeal spared neither age nor sex. In January 1863, Truesdale captured a man attempting to sneak past the pickets. In his possession was a letter written by a Mrs. Tindall of Nashville to her husband who was a captain in Wheeler's cavalry command. In her letter,

Mrs. Tindall noted that 15,000 men had passed through Nashville on their way to reinforce Rosecrans. General McCook, she noted, had gone North on leave of absence, as had several other generals. This meant that despite the arrival of reinforcements, Rosecrans was not intending to go on the offensive since his commanding officers were heading north on leave. Mrs. Tindall also sent her husband newspaper clippings and even offered to try to get a pass so she could bring him more information.

Truesdale arrested Mrs. Tindall and placed her under confinement in her own home. Soon after her arrest, in keeping with the accepted practice of the time, she was permitted to go south into Confederate occupied territory, supposedly to stay. In July 1863, Truesdale noted Mrs. Tindall was back in Nashville after having spent several months with Confederate forces. Truesdale was convinced that Mrs. Tindall was a spy who should be sent beyond the lines of the Union army and not allowed to return.

After the matter had been referred from Army Headquarters to District Headquarters an order was issued to Captain Wythe of the Provost Guard in Nashville to arrest Mrs. Tindall. As a result, she "was arrested today by order and paroled. From information received she was arrested last winter on the charges of sending the letter mentioned within to her husband by Colonel Truesdale and by him released. She received a pass from Genl Mitchell to go to Louisville. Learning that her husband was within eight miles of that place she went to him and south with him to McMinnville. On entering our lines she reported to me. I told her she would have to take the oath or be sent south. She was to return next morning but was taken prisoner and is now in Camp Chase. The above statement is made of the lady concerned by her mother."[24] Camp Chase in Columbus, Ohio, was one of the more notorious Northern prison camps, though no prison camp in either the North or the South was a health resort. It is not generally known that Southern civilians were sent to Prisoner of War camps, but the provost records clearly reveal that Southern civilians, including women, were incarcerated in these camps. Mrs. Tindall would not be the only Southern woman to suffer as a result of desiring to be near her husband. Mrs. Hugh McCrea, also of Nashville, had her own tale of misfortune recorded in the provost records.

On January 13, 1864, Colonel James L. Selfridge of the 46th Pennsylvania Volunteers reported apprehending Mrs. McCrea as she entered Union lines near Decherd, Tennessee. She was accompanied by her six children. Mrs. McCrea had come from the Confederate lines near Dalton, Georgia. The intrepid traveler had ventured across the rugged mountain terrain of North Alabama to Decatur where she crossed the Tennessee River. Avoiding Union patrols, she came into Union lines to remove personal property from her home. After securing her property, Mrs. McCrea intended to return to Confederate territory where she would again run the risk of arrest since she had been refused a pass through Southern lines to come to Tennessee. Colonel Selfridge was of the opinion that a great number of people followed the route used by Mrs. McCrea and asked what action should be taken in her case. Army Headquarters replied that the baggage and person of Mrs. McCrea was to be searched and that she was then to be sent south beyond the lines of the army. Any correspondence found in her possession was to be sent to the provost marshal in Nashville.[25]

The effectiveness of the Union naval blockade caused the Confederacy to be starved for many manufactured goods. The shortage of even the most common materials for making clothes was evident in the letter written by Dr. Blackmore to his wife, cited earlier. While those who attempted to run the naval blockade became figures of romantic legend or fiction, similar to Rhett Butler of *Gone with the Wind* fame, they also faced death or imprisonment for their attempt to aid the Confederacy and make enormous profits. An overlooked aspect of the war was the running of the land blockade by which the Union tried to choke off the flow of goods that were useful to the Confederate war effort, goods which often followed the corridor of the N&C Railroad. Many of those running the land blockade were far from romantic figures; they were quite ordinary people with an extraordinarily daring spirit. Some of them were strong Confederates despite having only a brief residency in the South. Clara Judd of Winchester, Tennessee, is one such case.

January 13, 1863

Capt Wm M. Wiles, Provost Marshal General, 3rd Army Corps

The following is the substance of the testimony elicited in the case of Mrs Clara Judd, arrested by the Army Police on charges of attempting to carry through the lines articles contraband of war, such as quinine, morphine, nitrate of silver, besides other goods & one knitting machine carried as a pattern, which articles were found to have been purchased by her and brought within these army lines upon a pass obtained under false pretenses.

Mrs Judd is the widow of an Episcopal Clergyman, who used to live in Winchester, Tennessee. He died some two years since leaving a large family of seven children. Mrs Judd passed through our lines with permission to take their youngest children to Minnesota from which the family originally comes. She took them there leaving them with a sister, she herself returning, passed through our lines to the rebel army. One of her oldest boys has found employment in the rebel establishments at Atlanta, Georgia. During her absence her premises were seized on by the Confederates & her children remaining were taken by this young man to Atlanta. In the autumn of 1862 she returned to Winchester went thence to Atlanta, claims to have received some five hundred dollars southern from her son, which she employed for money current in the south. She also received funds from persons who desired her to purchase articles from the north for them. Having thus provided herself, she came through our lines & was under her representations that she wished to go to her children in Minnesota granted a pass north. She states that from the conversation of officers of the Confederate service whom she met on the cars going from Atlanta to Murfreesboro she learned that it was the intention of John Morgan to strike at our rail road communications near Galatin at a certain time. She found a traveling companion in the person of a Mr Forsyth northbound. She went as far as Louisville & Jeffersonville or New Albany procuring the goods specified, returned on a pass to Gallatin. She states that her intention was to stop at Gallatin & set up the knitting machine & manufacture stockings for a living, her object in doing so being that she would be near her children in Atlanta & that she supposed it would be lawful for her to hold her goods in expectation that the enemy might reoccupy the country & that she would thus fall into their lines. it appears that she was tolerably well informed because about the time she expected it Morgan did make an attempt on Gallatin & shortly afterwards broke the road above there.

It is respectfully submitted that she is a dangerous women to remain in these lines — that she is probably a spy as well as a smuggler — that cases of this kind being of frequent occurrence by females that example should be made & that as there is at present no proper tribunal for her especial trial or proper place of imprisonment at Nashville that she be committed to the Military Prison at Alton in the State of Illinois for trial.

It is well to state further that Mrs Judd represents her son at Atlanta to be a skillful mechanic and that it was her intention to furnish him with the knitting machine for the purpose of manufacturing others from it taken as a pattern.

She has admitted since her imprisonment that she bore important dispatches on her person from General Bragg to persons north.

> Very Respectfully, Your Obt Servt
> John Hitch, Provost Judge
> Endorsed, William Truesdale, Chief of Army Police[26]

Mrs. Judd was sentenced to the Military Prison at Alton. The commanding officer of the prison, Colonel Jesse Hildebrand, noted on January 23,1863, that Mrs. Judd had arrived and that he had no decent place to keep her. He was providing board for her at a private house adjacent to the prison grounds for the cost of $2.00 per week. On May 11, Mrs. Judd gave a lengthy statement and claimed to have been tricked into smuggling and that her only motive had been to make enough money to pay her debts. On August 6, Mrs. Judd was released from confinement and sent to Minnesota for the duration of the war. Four of her children were in Minnesota with her parents while three others were employed in the government factory in Atlana producing Confederate uniforms.[27]

Sometimes the smuggling was on a very large scale, as the Confederates took advantage of the Union army's inability to occupy every foot of the area from which the main Confederate forces had been expelled. By the fall of 1863, the Confederate Army of Tennessee was besieging Chattanooga, but West and Middle Tennessee were considered to be Union territory. Yet, in a small, unoccupied pocket not far southwest of the line of the N&C, the Confederates were still hard at work moving cloth south. John Wortham, a prominent Union supporter in Shelbyville, Tennessee, and an officer in a Union regiment, wrote to General Gordon Granger on November 12, 1863, that a "reliable" citizen had just returned from a visit to Lawrence County, Tennessee, where he had found the cotton factories operating at full force manufacturing cloth for the Confederate government. Lawrence County had a Union garrison to its southwest at Florence, Alabama, on the Tennessee

River; other Union soldiers were in Nashville to the north, and the main Union army was east-northeast along the line of the N&C railroad. Despite being surrounded by Union forces, three hundred Confederate cavalry patrolled the county and protected the mills while secondary rural roads were used to send cloth south to Alabama and on to Georgia.[28] This was much the same route followed by Mrs. Hugh McCrea. Clearly, the Union was not successful in shutting down Confederate smuggling across the land blockade.

Even as the war entered its final weeks, the effort continued to gather goods in the area of the N&C and move them south for Confederate use.

> Maj John O. Cravens, AAGenl
>
> Sir
>
> I have the honor of making the following statement of facts in regard to one Parson Trimble, the husband of Mrs E. M. Trimble. On or about the first of Out 1864 I was on scout with orders from Maj Gen Milroy in Lincoln County after bands of bushwhackers that was stealing from the country.
>
> I recd information of a band that was comdg by James Whitman a brother of Mrs Trimble and that he made Parson Trimbles house his Hd Qrs. Taking my command and moved through the woods and fields and reached Mr Trimbles about 8 O'clock at night and picketed the roads so that I could catch them. I had not been there a long time before one of Whitmans men rode up and was taken in by Mrs Trimble and her sister Mrs Woosley. Heard them talking and I walked up. I was hailed by Mrs Trimble or her sister who came on out to the yard fence and demanded the countersign. When we got close enough for them to see that we were federals one of them remarked that we were Yankees and were on the loose. I placed a guard around the house and Mr Trimble began to make his escape and was caught and brought back and placed

under guard with Mr Elijah Woosley — it was not long after they were under guard until this band of bush-whackers rode up and was fired on and two of them killed. They had supper prepared at Mr Trimbles for at least ten men. I left Capt Chasteen with four men to guard the house and I taken the command some few miles to camp for the night and some time during the night Trimble and Woosley made their escape & Chasteen set fire to every thing that had a roof to it on the place there was nothing taken but a few womens clothing that was taken out by Mrs Trimble and Woosley and as for Parson Trimble loyalty Jeff Davis is a more loyal man to day than Parson Trimble he was a bushwhacker and a cotton burner in 1862 and he has been arrested twice to my knowledge.

I am respectfully

John Wortham Maj 5 Tenn Cav

P.S. The bacon 2700 lbs was taken by my order as I had information that Mr Trimble and Woosley had been get-ting up bacon for the rebel army during Hoods raid in Lincoln county and they could get this bacon out and you ordered me to get supplies from the country to subsist my men on. Mr Jas H Thompson came with Mrs Trimble to me to get a receipt for the bacon and to get clear of them I gave her a receipt for it knowing at the same time that she could get no vouchers for the bacon.

John Wortham Major 5 Tenn Cav[29]

The practice of smuggling goods was not something new for Parson Trimble. First Lieutenant W. R. Vaughn, 5th Ten-nessee Cavalry, U.S., swore before the provost that during the fall of 1863, Parson Trimble, his wife, and a neighbor named Elijah Woosley were engaged in smuggling bacon and other contraband goods across Elk River in the area south of the N&C. The area from the Elk River near Fayetteville south to the Tennessee River and on to Sand Mountain in Alabama swarmed with Confederate guerrillas. This route was followed by couriers, spies, and contraband goods making their way south. Vaughn said Trimble and Woosley had four wagon loads of bacon hidden near New Market, Alabama, but these goods were discovered by a Union patrol and confiscated. Trimble and Woosley had been arrested at that time but both were later released. It was Vaughn's opinion that Mrs. Trimble was a "bitter rebel" and was probably the instigator of the whole smuggling operation.[30]

The 5th Tennessee Cavalry was a locally raised Union regiment. Their actions clearly indicate that no war is as bitter as a true civil war in which neighbors had the chance to settle old grudges with neighbors, and to create new grudges along the way. One does not suspect that Major Wortham, Captain Chasteen, Lieutenant Vaughn, or any other member of the 5th Tennessee would have been found worshiping in Parson Trimble's church once the war was over. Burning everything "that had a roof on it" in attempts to stop the smuggling of goods south was not designed to make for smooth relations in the years to come.

One of the unusual features of life in the occupied South was that a person needed an official permit to purchase groceries and household supplies. One purpose of this system was to prevent civilians from stockpiling goods which could be sent south as opportunity offered. Such informal smuggling happened often enough that the Union army dealt severely with anyone suspected of engaging in the practice. This meant that a civilian who had permission to purchase goods but carelessly lost the receipt could potentially be suspected to be a smuggler. In Franklin County, Tennessee, James McAnally found himself on trial for this very matter in October 1864.

CHARGE FIRST: Smuggling goods through the lines of the Federal Army.

Specification: In this, that the said citizen James McAnally, of Franklin Co., Tenn, on or about the 10th day of May, 1864, at Dechard, Franklin County Tennessee, did, by affidavit, then and there duly swear that said goods were for family use only, and did procure goods and take them to his house with intent to sell them and otherwise dispose of them to persons in arms, and to persons aiding and abetting the rebellion against the Government of the United States.

CHARGE SECOND: Fraud

Specification 1st: In this, that said citizen James McAnally of Franklin Co. Tenn., on or about the 10th day of May, 1864, at Dechard, Franklin County, Tennessee, did procure a permit to purchase about fifteen dollars ($15.00) worth of goods, on his affidavit that they were family use only, and then did purchase about sixty-five ($65.00) dollars worth, and with intent to defraud the Government of the United States, did state that his permit was for the entire purchase.

Specification 2d: In this, that said citizen James McAnally, of Franklin County, Tenn, between the 10th and 31st days of May, 1864, near Dechard, Tenn., did sell, barter, and otherwise dispose of goods purchased under his affidavit that they were for family use only, which affidavit was made with intent to defraud and deceive the United States authorities at Dechard, Tenn.

CHARGE THIRD: PERJURY

Specification: In this, that the said citizen, James McAnally, of Franklin County, Tenn., on or about the 10th day of May, 1864, did for the purpose of procuring goods for contraband purposes, falsely swear that they were for his own family use.

Much to his relief, no doubt, McAnally was able to prove his innocence and was declared "Not Guilty" of all charges and specifications and acquitted by the Commission.[31]

Not all of the smuggling activity originated in the South. Some Northern civilians were motivated more by profit than patriotism, and took advantage of the high prices for scarce goods in the South in order to make money. This became so common that a ban was placed on the sale of gunpowder throughout the middle west. From the Headquarters of the Department of the Ohio, General Orders No. 72 stated:

> It having been ascertained that a large traffic in arms, powder, lead, and percussion caps is carried on at numerous points within the limits of this Department for purposes and uses disloyal to the Government of the United States, the provisions of General Orders No. 20 of the 14th inst from these Headquarters, prohibiting the sale of arms and munitions of war, are extended to embrace the limits of the Department.

> Permits to purchase may be obtained of the Military commander of the city or town where the sale is made; or if there be no such Military Commander in the place, then of the Military Commander of the city or town nearest to the place where the sale is made, or of the Commanding Officer of a District within the Department, upon the purchasers giving such security to the officer granting the permits as he shall deem sufficient that they will not sell, barter, give, or convey any such arms, or munitions of war, to any person disloyal to the Government of the United States, or to any person who will use such articles for purposes disloyal to the Government of the United States, or to any person from whom such articles shall pass into the possession of either of the above mentioned classes.

> Persons violating this order will be liable to arrest and trial, and the forfeiture to the United States of any and all munitions of war in their possession.

> The civil authorities and all loyal citizens are invited to aid the military authorities in carrying this order into effect.

> By Command of Maj General Wright
> N.H. McLean AAG & Chief of Staff[32]

The corridor of the N&C took on great military significance as the Civil War progressed. The railroad became a vital link in the Anaconda Strategy as the Union armies were forced to protect the rails even as the Confederate forces found it more and more important to break them. The conflict and unsettled conditions surrounding the transportation facility also allowed scouts, spies, and smugglers free reign. All those involved in the defense of the N&C railroad, from commanding general to mere privates, would have to fight hard to carry out their assignment. Their fight would become an unknown war fought on an unknown battlefield.

2

An Unknown Struggle

The defense of the N&C Railroad was an absolute necessity for the North since future Union advances depended on the possession of a functioning rail route. The first defenders of the N&C would be the front-line troops of the Army of the Cumberland who had just experienced a grand success in the Tullahoma campaign. With fewer than six hundred casualties, Rosecrans had pushed Bragg's Army of Tennessee out of Middle Tennessee, and positioned himself to occupy the critical rail junction town of Chattanooga, carrying the war to the front gate of Georgia. Now it was time for Rosecrans to consolidate his gains. The Union commander soon learned that the retreat of the Army of Tennessee had not cleared the region of armed and dangerous rebels. Major General Alexander McCook wrote from his headquarters at Winchester to Major General Philip Sheridan, whose headquarters was a few miles away at Cowan, to say, "You had better be on your guard. If there are Rebels in the cove they belong to Gurley who murdered my brother. Stanley reports that Gurley is in the mountains."[1]

McCook was referring to an event which had occurred a year earlier. Following the battle of Shiloh in April 1862, Union forces began to push out of Nashville toward Chattanooga. A brigade of these troops, commanded by Brigadier Robert L.

McCook, pushed south of the main line of advance along the N&C, moving south toward Huntsville, Alabama. McCook was not feeling well during much of the advance and was, on this occasion, riding in an ambulance. Toward the end of the day, near New Market, Alabama, the general ordered the ambulance driver to move ahead of the column of troops to find a place to bivouac for the night. The ambulance had drawn about four hundred yards ahead of the advance guard when it was ambushed by a party of eight men and McCook was killed.

The party which ambushed McCook was a detachment of the 4th Alabama Cavalry under the command of Captain Franklin "Frank" Gurley. Gurley's company served as an independent unit under the overall command of General Albert Sidney Johnston in early 1862. Later that year the regiment was placed under General Nathan Bedford Forrest. When the Tullahoma campaign brought the Union forces back to Middle Tennessee, Captain Gurley requested that he be allowed to return to his home area along the Alabama-Tennessee line and begin guerrilla operations against the Union rear. This request was granted and Gurley's unit provided scouts and guides for the area between the Tennessee River and Murfreesboro, Tennessee. Gurley was captured in late 1863 and his unit would be commanded by Lieutenant R. Manston until the end of the war.[2] Gurley was held as a prisoner of war until the Confederate surrender and was then placed on trial for the death of General McCook. Gurley and his men were regularly enlisted in an organized Confederate cavalry unit which served, on orders, in the regular Confederate service. Robert McCook knew Gurley's unit was active in the area he was traversing; indeed, one reason for his being there was to find and to defeat Gurley. Yet the general disregarded ordinary security precautions to travel in advance of his column without a proper escort, and, as a result of his carelessness, was ambushed. Perhaps the fact that McCook was killed in a skirmish where eight men dared operate in the face of a brigade caused the death to be called murder. Of course, the political influence of the McCook family helped arouse public opinion over the death of the general and to demonize his killer. However, the point should be well taken that war in the unknown struggle waged behind the lines would be deadly, personal, and bitter.

Also present in the newly occupied area were civilians with skills so valuable to the Confederacy that it became Union policy to apprehend these persons and to treat them as if they were POWs. R. P. Jackson, acting as provost marshal at Bridge-port, Alabama, reported on August 31, 1863, that he had just captured eight men, all of them miners. The men were being sent to the rear as prisoners. Two of these men, Horace Pyborn and William Birchfield, worked in saltpeter mines while the other six were coal miners.[3] Saltpeter, or nitrate, was a major ingredient in the black powder used in Civil War-era weap-ons. It was frequently manufactured by digging guano from caves where bats roosted, leaching water through the guano, and boiling down the water. Obviously, workers helping to produce ammunition for the Confederacy were valid targets for the Union forces, but it should be noted that coal miners also played a crucial role. All coal, at the time of the war, was used in industry since railroad trains did not yet have the fire-box draft to burn coal successfully. Confederate industry had become a significant enough factor in the war to make crip-pling the industrial fuel supply a military objective.

The unsettled conditions caused by military actions, the breakdown of civil law, and the partial and imperfect applica-tion of martial law allowed citizens an opportunity to settle old grudges under the guise of aiding one side or the other. One of the most notorious units out to settle old scores with neighbors, and to make money in the process, was a unit of Union "Scouts" commanded by Calvin Brixey. This erstwhile Union captain, and most of his men, had supported the Con-federacy so long as that was the dominant power in the Middle Tennessee area. With the arrival of the Union forces, Brixey quickly changed sides and became a terror to the whole countryside. This would, unfortunately, be the record of many of the "Galvanized Yankees," units of Tennesseans raised locally for Union service. The record of many of these units proves clearly that there is no war more bitter than a true civil war where neighbors confront neighbors.

Near Pelham, Tenn Sept 1st A.D. 1863

Genrl G.D. Wagner

Dear Sir we the undersigned citizens of Grundy county and vicinity of Pelham beg leave to state our grievances as a people to you and hope fully ask that you take such steps as you may think the nature of the case and circumstances demands. Since your departure from the neighborhood the company recently organized under Capt Bricksy have assumed authority to arrest quiet citizens without any charge whatever have taken private property such as young horses and mules (not in any wanted for the service) and appropriated them to their own private use all of this to us seems unwarranted and wrong and hoping that we have some claims to protection from the Federal Government especially against men who have gone further in the Rebellion than any of us, joined that army without any compulsion whatever and when their old associates have to quit the country they throw themselves upon the mercies of the Federal Government, join the Loyal Army and are now fortified in their assumption to deal with citizens and their property generally as they were ever to do with the property of hated Union men, as they were pleased to style them while in the Rebel ranks. But we do not allude to the entire company for some men in it have never been identified with the rebellion nor do we believe they have engaged in the above mentioned practices, but a number have. The proof of which can be established beyond question. Hoping that you will at an early day give the subject the action you think it demands and make some disposition of the said Bricksys Company which will give relief to the country. We have the honor to be

Very Respectfully Your Obt Servants.[4] There are 24 signatures on the document.

Armed and dangerous rebels continued to take a small, but deadly, toll of the occupying force. Unlike Gurley's men, who were regularly enrolled Confederate soldiers, some of the opposition came from disgruntled civilians who took matters into their own hands. Two such were John W. Johnson and Alexander P. Anderson who paid a price for their opposition to the Union army. On September 4, 1863, these two men had fired on two U.S. soldiers at a point about three miles north of the village of Hillsboro, Tennessee. The village was located on a major road crossing the Cumberland range and received a steady stream of military traffic moving southeast toward Chattanooga. Three miles north of Hillsboro a local road crossed a creek, a spot where travellers would pause to water horses or, perhaps, remove their shoes before wading the creek.

The provost records do not reveal why two U.S. soldiers were present in this area away from the main road, but they were ambushed by Johnson and Anderson who killed one of the soldiers and wounded the other. Both soldiers were then searched and robbed. Somehow the two civilians were apprehended and brought to trial before a military commission. Johnson was found guilty and was sentenced

> To be hung by the neck until he is dead, at such time and place as may be designated by the General Commanding the Department or District.The proceedings, findings, and sentence of the Commission in the Case of John W. Johnson, citizen, having been approved by the proper commanders, and the record forwarded for the action of the President of the United States, who approves the sentence, and directs that it be duly executed.[5]

Alexander P. Anderson was found guilty, but with mitigating circumstances, and was sentenced to five years in the state penitentiary.[6]

By late August 1863, the Army of the Cumberland was moving into North Georgia as the maneuvering began which would end in the battle of Chickamauga. By late September, Rosecrans' command was trapped in Chattanooga and the cavalry of the Army of Tennessee, under the command of Joseph Wheeler, was set loose to wreak havoc on the Union supply lines. Wheeler had only limited success on this raid. Rosecrans had gotten part of his cavalry out of Chattanooga so as to oppose Wheeler. The first of 16,000 troops from the Army of the Potomac, the corps of Slocum and Hooker, arrived soon after Wheeler started his incursion and these troops reestablished Union dominance in Middle Tennessee. One division of Slocum's Corps was commanded by General Alpheus Williams who had distinguished himself by his defense of the Union right flank at Gettysburg. He would soon become the commander, Military Sub-District #1, Defenses of the Nashville and Chattanooga Railroad.

Williams was born in Deep River, Connecticut, on September 20, 1810. By age 17 he was an orphan who had inherited $75,000. Williams attended Yale after receiving his inheritance and then spent some time studying law. From 1831 to 1836 he traveled in Europe and America before settling down in what was then a "boom town," Detroit, Michigan. In 1839 Williams married a widow, Jane Hereford Pierson, who died only ten years later, leaving him a widower with three children: Irene, Charles Larned, and Mary. Williams entered politics in Detroit, became probate judge for Wayne County, served as president of the Bank of St. Clair, and purchased the *Detroit Advertiser*. He served as postmaster of Detroit beginning in 1849 and was also involved in various militia organizations. In 1861 Williams helped prepare the Michigan militia for service and was promoted to the rank of brigadier of U.S. Volunteers in August of that year. He was never promoted to a higher rank, although he served competently.[7]

General Williams experienced a week's delay in getting his forces into position along the railroad because of guerrilla activity. Once his men were in place, Williams moved to establish control over the area. Of particular concern to him was the 2,200-foot-long tunnel at Cowan, Tennessee. When the tunnel was constructed, three air shafts had been driven up to the crest of the mountain. These shafts were frequently used by Confederate cavalry and guerrillas to roll rocks down onto the tracks to block trains. There were also constant rumors of Confederate cavalry moving to attack isolated posts along the rail line and its branches. It was Williams' responsibility to guard the railroad from Tullahoma to halfway between the villages of Cowan and Tantalon, a total of 22 miles of track that included the vulnerable tunnel. With this expanse of territory under his command Williams noted that he was only able to guard bridges, tunnels, culverts, and water tanks.[8] His duties would soon become more demanding but without the addition of more troops. Originally Williams' troop disposition would be to place General Thomas H. Ruger's brigade from Tullahoma to the Elk River, with General Joseph F. Knipe's brigade guarding from the Elk River to Cowan. Division headquarters was at Decherd. By November 11, 1863, however, Williams had been given responsibility for all the railroad from Murfreesboro, Tennessee, to Bridgeport, Alabama, a distance of over 90 miles. This made the task of supervision almost impossible. "The road is in a bad condition and the engines are old and worthless. it is a good days work to get forty miles covered,"[9] the general noted. By November 20 Williams had moved his headquarters.[10] This location was more centrally located and established Tullahoma as the Union headquarters for the Defenses of the N&C Railroad for the remainder of the war.

General Williams was constantly in motion, inspecting the defenses along his 90 miles of track because "if important

Blockhouse on the N&C Railroad guarding the bridge over Duck River near Normandy, Tennessee

Tennessee State Museum Collection,
Photography by June Dorman

General Alpheus Williams, commander of Military Sub-District #1, 1863–64

Courtesy Library of Congress

bridges are lost the whole army goes up, as they are just able
to live now. So the responsibility is immense, without any possible credit. The country is full of guerrilla parties and the Rebel
cavalry are always menacing right and left to pounce in upon
a weak point."[11]

Williams was neither impressed with his duties nor with
the place where he had to carry out these duties. The town of
Tullahoma, which became his headquarters, he described as
consisting of about one hundred

> straggling houses of faded paint and retrograde look.
> Judge Catron of the Supreme Court has a neat summer
> cottage in the suburbs, but it is badly soiled by the occu-
> pation of soldiers. The town is dolorous . . . thin, slabby,
> and shabby houses scattered about, with broken windows
> and a deserted air. The people are like the houses, poor
> white trash. The Negro is the only gay dog, keeping up
> dances every night and having a good time at a cheap
> rate . . . The people are disgusting: the mere scum of hu-
> manity, poor, half-starved, ignorant, stupid, and treach-
> erous. The women all dip snuff. You must stay here and
> move through the country to see how many there are
> vastly inferior to the Negro in common sense, shrewd-
> ness, and observation, and in the comforts of life. Let us
> not grieve for the Southern Negro as much as for the poor
> Southern White man—covered with vermin and rags, and
> disgusting with the evidence of a cureless 'Scotch fiddle'
> (scabies) which they dig at continuously.[12]

But as poor as the countryside seemed to Williams, the woods
surrounding Tullahoma and the area for which he was responsible were equally as rich in guerrillas.

Some of these guerrilla units consisted of men who were
from Middle Tennessee and who, when the Tullahoma campaign led to Confederate retreat, deserted their commands
to stay behind in an attempt to protect their homes. The 5th

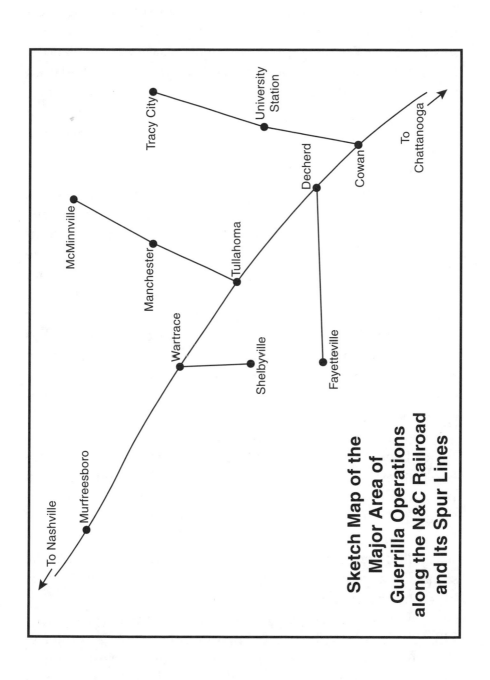

Sketch Map of the Major Area of Guerrilla Operations along the N&C Railroad and Its Spur Lines

To Nashville

Murfreesboro

McMinnville

Manchester

Wartrace

Shelbyville

Tullahoma

Fayetteville

Decherd

Cowan

University Station

Tracy City

To Chattanooga

Tennessee Cavalry was the Union unit which caused the guerrillas the greatest concern. Most of the men in this unit came from Middle Tennessee, indeed it was occasionally called the 1st Middle Tennessee because several of its companies had been recruited from the area of Shelbyville and Bedford County. The 5th had played a significant role in the Union capture of Shelbyville in June 1863, after which the regiment became a part of the occupying Union force.

If the 5th Tennessee seemed to be out to settle old scores it is probably because the families of many of its members had suffered at the hands of their Confederate neighbors in 1861 and 1862. On August 2, 1863, Brigadier W. C. Whitaker, commanding the 1st Division, Reserve Corps, Army of the Cumberland, said, "The Tennessee cavalry of Colonel Galbraith, the 5th Tennessee, is giving me excessive trouble, and worrying and plundering through the country whenever they go out. They are under no control or discipline at all as far as I can learn. Several instances have come to my attention of their insulting females."[13] It is likely that these females who were "insulted" included the wives and daughters of Confederate soldiers.

On the 14th and 15th of December 1863, the guerrillas struck back. On the 14th five men—William Lemmons, Cyrus Lee Cathey, Jesse B. Neeren, Thomas R. West, and Benjamin West—attacked Union supporters and soldiers near the village of Boons Hill, Tennessee, some few miles west of Fayetteville. In this foray Irwin C. McLean, a Union citizen, was killed and robbed of $2,200, a horse, and clothing. On the same day another Union supporter, Samuel J. Wakefield, was killed by the guerrilla band.

The next day the same five men struck near Shelbyville, killing William White, a citizen, and Grey Hyde, a soldier in the 5th Tennessee. Hyde's horse and weapons were taken as were those of another trooper in the 5th, William Smith, who escaped with his life. To round out the day, Newcomb Thompson lost 10 mules to the guerrillas. Other robberies of Union men were carried out on December 17. A month later, on January 15, 1864, the guerrillas attacked a forage train of two wagons on the Connellsville Road in Bedford County, drove off the guard, burned the wagons, and took the horses which pulled the wagons. The men were captured in February and tried by a military commission chaired by Colonel E. A. Curman, 13th New Jersey, found guilty, and

> The sentences of Death by hanging in the cases of William Lemmons, Cyrus Lee Cathie, Jesse B. Neeren, Thomas R. West and Benjamin F. West, citizens, having been approved by the President of the United States in Paragraph II General Court Martial Orders, War Dept., No. 87, will be carried into execution under the direction of Brigadier General Jno F. Miller, Comdg Post at Nashville, Tenn, upon Friday June 17 1864, between the hours of 10 A.M. and 4 P.M.[14]

Such reverses did not deter the guerrillas. In November 1863, a detachment was sent from Tullahoma out the Fayetteville road to forage in the vicinity of the village of Mulberry. This village, on the eastern edge of Lincoln County, was a hotbed of pro-Confederate sentiment. Presently the village has no more than 150 inhabitants, yet on the village green stands a monument dedicated to the "more than 300 soldiers from Mulberry who entered Confederate service." Those men who were not in military service had been quick to rally to oppose the invader as soon as the Union army entered their area at the conclusion of the Tullahoma campaign. Thomas P. Wells told the Union provost that on Monday, the 13th day of July 1863, he was riding out the Mulberry Pike with a neighbor, Squire Cunningham, when the pair met several well-armed and -equipped guerrillas about two miles west of Tullahoma. One of them, Joe Poe, was mounted on a horse that Wells recognized as having been stolen from his kinsman,

Parson Wells. Another member of the party was identified as
Bill Chasteen, also "strongly armed." The third was described
as "a short thick heavy stout man with long black hair cut round
dark skin dark eyes goatee had on a check shirt." The guerrillas inquired if any horses were grazing in the old fields and
where the pickets were stationed.[15]

Scouting the Union lines was only a preliminary activity.
With the passage of time the guerrillas grew bolder and were
ready to strike. The account of one such strike recorded in the
provost records paints a brutal picture of the savage nature of
the war behind the lines.

> Tullahoma, Dec 26, 1863
>
> Captain: I have the honor to report that, on the 23d
> inst, I sent a forage train into the neighborhood of Mul-
> berry Village, Lincoln County. The train was accompa-
> nied by a guard of 70 men under the command of First
> Lieutenant Porter, Company A, Twenty-seventh Indiana
> Volunteers. Lieutenant Porter was furnished with copies
> of General Orders No. 17, November 17, 1862, and Gen-
> eral Orders, No. 30, December 30, 1862, Department of
> the Cumberland, and also Special Orders, No. ___, of these
> headquarters, for instructions. At or near Mulberry Vil-
> lage, I am informed by Lieutenant Porter, he divided his
> train into four detachments and sent the several detach-
> ments onto different plantations, sending an equal guard
> with each detachment. This, I understand, was done for
> the purpose of facilitating the loading of the train. It was
> about 7 o'clock in the evening when that portion of the
> train which Lieutenant Porter was with finished loading
> and started into camp.
>
> The Lieutenant reports that while he was in the house
> receipting for the forage a part of the train went ahead
> and went into camp, leaving three wagons in the rear. He
> started to camp with these three wagons, distance about 2
> miles. He had with him 15 men as guard. When within

one-half mile of camp he discovered that the foremost wagon had got about 300 yards ahead of the other two. He went forward for the purpose of halting it. When he rode up he found the wagon stopped. Two men immediately rode up to him and presented pistols at his head and demanded his surrender. With this wagon was the teamster and wagon-master of the Ninth Ohio Battery, and 2 men who had helped to load the wagons, all unarmed except Lieutenant Porter. The guerrillas numbered but 4, and were armed. Lieutenant Porter, the wagon-master, and three men were immediately mounted and taken through a gate, passing about 200 yards up a creek and then into a corn-field; from there they were hurried forward, avoiding roads, &c, until about 1 o'clock in the morning. They were halted on the bank of Elk River, about 1 mile below where the Mulberry empties into it. A fire was built and their captors informed them that they were going to camp for the night.

Their hands were tied behind them; everything of value was taken from them. They were then drawn up in line 4 or 5 steps in front of their captors; one of them, who acted as leader, commanded "Ready"; the whole party immediately fired. One of the men was shot through the head and killed, as supposed, instantly; 3 were wounded. Lieutenant Porter was not hit, and immediately broke and ran. He was followed and fired at by one of the party three times. He reports that he saw that he would be overtaken, and changed his course and ran to the river and threw himself over a precipice into the water. Having succeeded in getting his hands loose, he swam to the opposite shore; was fired at five or six times while he was in the water. He secreted himself under the bank of the river. His captors swam their horses across the river and made search for him, but failed to find him. He afterward made his way up the river about three-fourths of a mile and swam back again. He lay in the woods the remainder of the night and the next day. On the night of the 24th he traveled about a mile and got to a house. The party sent out by me on yesterday brought him in. He is now lying in a critical condition owing to the exposure, cold, fatigue, &c.

He reports that he would know his captors should he see them again, one of whom is believed to be a man by the name of Tulley, living near Lynchburg; another a Bowne, who is a deserter from the rebel army and has been during the fall and winter with guerrillas. A third man rode a bay stallion and is known to the citizens of Mulberry; his name I have not yet learned.

The men who were shot were immediately thrown into the river, one of whom was supposed to have been killed, and one, from the nature of the wounds and his appearance after the body was recovered, is supposed to have been drowned. The hands of these two men were tied behind them when taken out of the river, the other two men succeeded in loosing their hands and got out of the river, one of whom has died since; the other is now in the hospital at this place; wound not considered necessarily mortal.

The names of the murdered men are as follows: John W. Drought and George W. Jacobs, Twenty-second Wisconsin Volunteers (the men were temporarily attached to the Ninth Ohio Battery); Newell E. Orcutt, Ninth Ohio Battery, wounded and since died; James W. Foley, Ninth Ohio Battery, wounded and now in the hospital at this place. The three first named are men of families in destitute circumstances. The latter has an aged mother destitute, dependent upon him for support.

S. Colgrove
Colonel, Commanding Post[16]

The response of the Union army was to send a detachment into the area for the purpose of arresting the culprits. The expedition was not successful.

Lt Col Muse, Asst Adgt Genl 12th Corps

Col I have the honor to report that in obedience to orders from Corps H Qrs a detachment of men (mounted) was on the 29th inst sent into the neighborhood of Mulberry for the purpose of arresting guerrillas & etc. The detachment returned last night & reported the results of their operations. No one who can be identified with the recent murder of the men of the 9th Ohio Battery was arrested. Tolley, supposed to be the leader of the gang, made his escape although they are yet looking on the day our party arrived there. Search was made in the neighborhood for other leading guerrillas but without success. John Tolley, the father of Burton Tolley, was arrested and brought in according to instructions. Also, Thomas Baley, Doctor Philander Whitier & Newton Whitier these men have been reported by authority considered worthy of credit to be guerrillas and especially that they have harbored, fed, and succored them, they are now in the guardhouse awaiting further orders.

On yesterday morning after the train had started home the Lieut reports a Negro man led him to the barn of John Tolley which was burned down. The negro is a man that had been working in the area and was not connected with the post or with the party that was sent out, the negro was arrested and is now detained in the guard house.

The Lieut in command of the detachment was instructed that in case he could not get positive proof of John Tolley's guilt or the old man's participation in the crime of murdering the men to burn the house and outbuildings of John Tolley. He reports upon this subject that he failed in getting proof sufficient to justify this course & therefore did not execute that part of the order and gave no command or authority for the same. The burning of the barn was not authorized.

Contemporary view of Mulberry, Tennessee

Photograph by Author

**Confederate monument to
the three hundred soldiers
from the village**

Photograph by Author

Lieut S. Loring learned from the people down there that the negro had threatened to burn it before he ran away from them, alleging that Tolley had moved his wife and children south. The negro was the property of the Widow Browne, niece of John Tolley.

I respectfully suggest that the one means to brake up and destroy the guerrillas in that neighborhood is to send a sufficient force of Cavalry in there entirely disconnected with a foraging party and take sufficient time for that purpose and scour the whole country as far south as Huntsville. I suppose two hundred mounted men would be sufficient if that force could be placed at my disposal I am willing to take command of it and go in person. I have every confidence that I could efficiently make it up.

> Respectfully Your Obedient Servant
> Silas Colgrave, Col Comdg Post[17]

The practice of taking prisoner civilians who were thought to harbor and feed guerrillas and holding them hostage was a new attempt to control the population. The guerrillas proved to be too slippery to catch, so the best hope of driving them out of the country was to destroy the infrastructure which supported the guerrilla bands, if of course, the right civilians could be arrested. And if such action did not make the supporters of the guerrillas even more determined to aid those who pestered their Yankee tormentors.

The action toward the unnamed Negro man is also informative of the attitudes of Midwestern soldiers toward slaves. The Emancipation Proclamation had been in effect for a full year at this point in the war, but the Army of the Cumberland and Slocum's Corps of the Army of the Potomac were not much interested in freeing slaves. Their overriding concern was to maintain order, and in this case, to prevent the Negro man from exacting private vengeance against a slave owner who had separated him from his family.

Since the detachment sent to Mulberry was not able to catch the guerrillas who had ambushed the forage train, General George Thomas decided to apply another form of deterrence. In General Orders No. 6 Thomas first described the killing of the men and then ordered:

> For these atrocious and cold-blooded murders, equaling in savage ferocity any ever committed by the most barbarous tribes on the continent, committed by rebel citizens of Tennessee, it is ordered that the property of all other rebel citizens living within a circuit of 10 miles of the place where these men were captured be assessed, each in his due proportion, according to his wealth, to make up the sum of $30,000, to be divided among the families who were dependent upon the murdered men for support, as follows:
>
> Ten thousand dollars to be paid to the widow of John W. Drought of North Cape, Racine County, Wis., for the support of herself and two children.
>
> Ten thousand dollars to be paid to the widow of George W. Jacobs, of Delavan, Walworth County, Wis., for the support of herself and one child.
>
> Ten thousand dollars to be divided between the aged mother and sister of Newell E. Orcutt, of Burton, Geauga County, Ohio.
>
> Should the persons assessed fail, within one week after notice shall have been served upon them, to pay in the amount of their tax in money, sufficient of their personal property shall be seized and sold at public auction to make up the amount.
>
> Maj. Gen. H. W. Slocum, U.S. Volunteers, commanding Twelfth Army Corps, is charged with the execution of this order.
>
> The men who committed these murders, if caught, will be summarily executed, and any persons executing them will be held guiltless and will receive the protection of

this army; and all persons who are suspected of having aided, abetted, or harbored these guerrillas will be immediately arrested and tried by military commission.

By command of Major-General Thomas[18]

After camping for several days in the vicinity of Mulberry, the brigade returned with the money, and ironically, was ambushed by guerrillas who killed two men who had gotten in advance of the main body of the brigade. In 1866 the actions of General Slocum were still in debate since his men had exceeded their orders in regard to Mulberry.

> Mulberry Lincoln County Tenn
> July 13th 1866

General

Pursuant to General Orders No. 6 dated HdQrs Dept of the Cumberland January 6th 1864, a tax of thirty thousand dollars was levied upon the people of the neighborhood for the killing of certain parties named therein. The amount actually collected was about sixty-six thousand dollars which the receipts of the Collecting Officer will show.

Two years and a half has elapsed since the killing took place and no evidence has been adduced implicating any one living in this county with the killing. I am therefore induced to inquire if that money can not be refunded? If not, can the excess of what your order called for be refunded? Were you aware that more than twice the amount called for in your order was collected?

An early answer is respectfully solicited.

I am General, Very Respectfully

J.H. Holman[19]

Throughout the records of the provost marshal instances of the seizure of valuable civilian property not suitable for military use and the subsequent disappearance of that property is documented. This record leads to the conclusion that systematic looting of the civilian population for the purpose of personal financial gain frequently took place behind Union lines in Middle Tennessee throughout the war. Alpheus Williams would write to his daughter, "The making of fortunes I do not understand. I could have made one here if I had consented to have sold my self-respect and the good name of my children to the third and fourth generation. While somebody makes $700,000, somebody else loses a corresponding sum."[20] Such actions had already reduced much of the area of Military Sub-District #1 to a wasteland and its inhabitants to poverty by the end of 1863. General Lovell Rousseau wrote:

> I desire to call attention to another matter. From impressments, legal and illegal, and from thefts, there are very few horses, mules, or oxen left on the farms, and the few that are left are almost worthless. At present there are many large farms without one serviceable work beast on the place. The farmers are afraid to purchase because of repeated impressments. Every mounted regiment that goes through the country takes what it pleases of stock &c, and pays what price, or none at all it likes. Between the loyal and disloyal no discrimination is made. Unless an order be made preventing future impressments and protecting the farmers, little or no crops will be produced.[21]

Williams could not concern himself with civilian welfare; he had his hands full with defending the railroad. Much confusion and many contradictory orders from Generals Hooker and Slocum were directed at Williams, who had the unfortunate situation of commanding territory which fell partly into each of these superior officers' sphere of command. Hooker had his headquarters at Chattanooga, and Slocum had his at Wartrace, which meant that Williams and his men were constantly marching and countermarching across the mountain at Cowan which separated the commands of Hooker and Slocum. In addition to travel which wore out men and horses, the railroad tracks near Cowan were blown up by a "torpedo," or primitive land mine. Williams complained in a letter home that his troops "now occupy small posts, just large enough to be gobbled up" by the guerrillas operating in the mountains. The whole situation was not to Williams' liking. "I dislike this railroad guarding in small posts. The whole country is full of small guerrilla bands who can get to the track and tear it up in spite of anything the infantry can do . . . Besides, the posts at important bridge are too small to defend themselves against serious attack."[22] Williams also said something which would prove to be an astute commentary on the quality of those who would follow him in the command of the defenses of the railroad and of the provost marshals who would exercise control over the civilian population: "In trying to give places to officers not wanted in the field a great many useless commands are carried out in the shape of military districts and independent posts."[23] The reason most of these officers were "not wanted in the field" was that they were incompetent.

The guerrilla who gave Williams the most trouble was not a man dedicated to the policy of guerrilla warfare, but a regular army officer who found himself cut off behind Union lines and decided to inflict all the damage he could until he had the opportunity to rejoin the Army of Tennessee. Colonel John M. Hughes had been a captain, and later a major, in the 25th Tennessee Infantry and had fought in all the campaigns and battles of the Army of Tennessee through Stones River in December 1862. At that battle he had been wounded and sent home to recover from his injuries. As he neared recovery he was assigned the light duties of recruiting and gathering up others who were also recovering from wounds or who had been allowed to go home on furlough. The Tullahoma campaign took place at this time and Hughes found himself behind Union lines. During the late summer and early fall of 1863, Hughes organized the men he had gathered and, on October 6 attacked Glasgow, Kentucky, where he captured 100 men, seized Union commissary stores and burned what he could not carry off, and mounted most of his men from horses that had been seized locally.[24] Building on this success, Hughes went on a campaign in the Cumberland Mountains of Kentucky and Tennessee, and captured Monticello, Kentucky, on November 27. Three days later he fought a rear guard action against the 1st Tennessee Cavalry, U.S. in which 13 Union soldiers were killed, 8 wounded, and 7 were captured while Hughes lost only 5 of his men. Hughes later led 200 men to capture Scottsville , Kentucky, where he captured 86 Union soldiers and 500 stand of arms while losing only one of his own men. He then attacked Livingston, Tennessee, and defeated the 13th Kentucky Cavalry, U.S.[25]

Despite the fact that Hughes was a regular army officer leading men he had sworn into regular Confederate service, he was still considered to be an outlaw by the Union authorities. Lieutenant Colonel James P. Brownlow of the 1st Tennessee Cavalry, U.S., said he would take no prisoners should he meet Hughes, and Brigadier General Hobson gave orders that no prisoners should be taken. Hughes complained of this treatment, saying he should not be placed in the same category as men such as Champ Ferguson, a notorious Confederate guerrilla.[26]

In January 1864, the weather was so severe that Hughes operated mainly against Union bushwhackers or "Tories," but in February he returned to his campaign. He again attacked Monticello, Kentucky, and then fought a skirmish with the pro-Union guerrilla band of "Tinker Dave" Beaty. At the end of February, Hughes fought a series of engagements around Sparta, Tennessee, with the Union 5th Tennessee Cavalry commanded by Colonel Robert Stokes. This unit also had said that no prisoners would be taken from Hughes' command, but Hughes lured the Tennessee Unionists into a skillful ambush and killed 47, wounded 13, and captured 4. Colonel Stokes complained that the country around Sparta was "infested with a great number of rebel soldiers and I have to fight for every ear of corn and blade of fodder I get."[27] That same month Hughes captured the town of Washington, Tennessee, took 65 prisoners, and broke up a company of recently formed Union home guards.

In March, Hughes' command lost a skirmish with their old opponents, the 5th Tennessee Cavalry, but went on to tear up the N&C near Tullahoma and capture a train of supplies. "About 60 Yankee soldiers were captured and 20 Yankee negroes killed." The train, and what supplies could not be carried off, were burned.[28]

By April, Hughes had returned to his regiment near Dalton, Georgia, taking out with him 95 recruits for the army. At any given time his band had numbered from 85 to as many as 300 men. He had killed and captured about 1,100 Union soldiers and had captured and destroyed 3,500 stand of arms which his own men could not use.[29]

Civilians were punished when they were in areas where guerrilla attacks occurred. The policy of punishing civilians who were thought to be friendly toward guerrillas was not limited to these areas. Too much enthusiasm for the Confederate cause could also bring unwanted attention from the Union authorities. Lieutenant Colonel P. H. Sturdevant of the 12th Army Corps, one of the Army of the Potomac units sent to Tennessee in the fall of 1863, was stationed at Shelbyville. That county seat town was noted for being antisecession and had so many pro-Union residents that the town was often called "Little Boston." But Colonel Sturdevant felt that an example should be made of those who supported the Confederacy. He complained to the Provost Headquarters in Tullahoma that permits had been issued to "disloyal citizens" to allow them to purchase groceries from the U.S. commissary. The colonel particularly singled out Mrs. R. W. Wallace whose husband was the cashier of one of the town's banks. Mr. Wallace had taken all the bank deposits and had gone south when U.S. forces appeared in June 1863. Miss Ann Wallace, daughter of the cashier, was also labeled as a rebel. Others whose loyalty was questioned included Miss M. Matthews, Miss V. Matthews, and Miss Selica Whitthorn, all members of prominent local families. The permits to purchase goods had been given to these women by Colonel Robert Galbraith, commander of the 1st Middle Tennessee Cavalry, U.S. Army. Colonel Galbraith was opposed to his neighbors' politics but, as a local resident, was unwilling to see women and children suffer. Colonel Sturdevant felt no compulsion against punishing the women. He insisted that the women be denied the opportunity to purchase groceries. His commanding officer, General Joseph Hooker, agreed and sent the recommendation forward to General George Thomas. The reply from Thomas said, "General Slocum will direct the Commissary at Shelbyville to stop the rations of these people."[30] Clearly, it was General Thomas' opinion that leaving these women without food would discourage support for the Confederacy generally, if not for the guerrillas around Shelbyville specifically. Later events would prove him wrong. But behind Union lines, pro-Confederate women were being recognized as valuable assets that helped keep the war going. A "hard war" policy which included women would be the response by the provost marshal to that recognition.

The policy of taking hostages soon extended beyond arresting those who were thought to be sympathetic to guerrillas to simply seizing someone in order to guarantee the good behavior of their neighbors. This practice began around the town of McMinnville, Tennessee, the county seat of Warren County. Although the practice was not condoned by General Orders No. 100 no official action was taken to stop hostage taking. Plagued by guerrillas operating from the mountains east of the town, the Union officer commanding McMinnville in Warren County, Tennessee, took action against Zenas Sanders and John Martin. H. C. Gilbert, colonel of the 19th Michigan

Infantry commanded the post at McMinnville. The town is surrounded by mountains and was tenuously linked to the main forces in Middle Tennessee by a single-track branch line of the N&C. Guerrillas frequently attacked the town itself with Union soldiers being killed in the streets, and guerrillas controlled a vital crossroads less than three miles from the Union lines. These guerrillas made constant depredations on the pro-Union citizens in the area.

In an attempt to protect the pro-Union population and also to suppress the guerrillas, Colonel Gilbert arrested Zenas Sanders and John Martin. When arresting them the colonel announced that he intended to hold them hostage for the lives and safety of the Unionist population. Both Sanders and Martin were wealthy men who supported secession, so Colonel Gilbert assumed they would have influence on other, less wealthy men who held similar political views and that their influence extended to the bands of marauders who were attacking Unionist residents in the area.

One of the two hostages, Zenas Sanders, was sent back to his home to actively pursue communications with the guerrillas, but he was ordered to report regularly to Union headquarters on his progress. It was stated bluntly to Mr. Sanders that he would be personally held responsible for any attacks made by guerrillas on his pro-Union neighbors. If any of his neighbors were driven from their homes, Sanders' house, barns, and other property would be destroyed and he, with his destitute family, would be driven out of Warren County.

John Martin was placed under the same threat but was held in the post stockade as a prisoner. Then the colonel added:

> Other citizens of secession proclivities residing near Mr Sanders and Mr Hawkins will be expected to cooperate actively in the work of pacifying the country and in case they fail to do so will in like manner with them be held reasonable for failure.

> Finally, I wish it to be distinctly understood that Rebel
> Citizens will be held responsible for all unlawful acts of
> guerrillas and bushwhackers in their neighborhoods and
> if Union men are to be driven away Rebels must go too,
> the game hereafter will not be all on one side.[31]

Colonel Gilbert decided to expand his policy of hostage taking and ordered the arrest of James M. Green. The charge against Green was harboring and encouraging a "gang of bushwhackers" who operated in northern and western Warren County. Indeed, Green was said to have a son who was a member of the gang. As was the case with Sanders and Martin, Green was told that

> Hereafter he will be in his own person and to the extent of his property be held responsible for the depredations of the bushwhackers. The damage they commit will be assessed upon his property and if possible collected.
>
> If Union men are driven from their homes Mr Green and his family must go too and he may depend upon it that his own personal safety as well as the further enjoyment of his property depends upon the breaking up of the gang.[32]

Reaching out yet again, Colonel Gilbert ordered the arrest of William Anderson who was accused of being a leading secessionist as well as a supporter of guerrillas. Anderson was thought to be responsible for assisting in the organization and operation of guerrillas in the Rocky Rim area of Warren County. The order for his arrest specifically states that he is being held as hostage for the safety of the "loyal" men of his neighborhood and that his property would be used to repay any Union supporter robbed by guerrillas.

Arrested at the same time as Anderson was Isaac Deaton. He was sent back to his neighborhood as a messenger to inform all Confederate supporters that their lives and property would be in danger as long as attacks were made on Union supporters. The reason for singling out Anderson and Deaton was that

> Inasmuch as the best Union men are always selected as victims by the marauders, the pleas of respect for liberty so urgently presented by Mr Anderson & wife will be of no avail. Only respectable rebels, men of influence & wealth are to be held responsible for further outrages.
>
> Mr Denton will assure such men that this is no idle talk—if necessary to ensure the safety of Union men every rebel plantation or abode helping him will be laid waste.[33]

The "get tough" policy did not work and guerrillas continued to be active throughout the area. On May 25, 1864, Captain I. N. Campbell reported contact with guerrillas not far from McMinnville. The captain said:

> On my return from escorting Major Rodgers, paymaster, to McMinnville, when near Cripple Creek, on Woodbury Pike, I heard of some guerrillas crossing the pike and going into the cedars. I followed them and overtook the party (five men, mounted and armed with carbines and revolvers) near the house of Jesse Beshears. They were drawn in line across the lane, but after exchanging one round fled to the cedars. We killed 1 of the party, but the balance succeeded in making their escape. They appeared to be loaded with goods, and undoubtedly belonged to the band of guerrillas that have been plundering in the vicinity of Shelbyville.[34]

Other bands of guerrillas were so active that an expedition had to be ordered out in an attempt to squelch them. Limited success was experienced in capturing and killing guerrillas, but a good deal of property was destroyed as a result of this expedition. The officer in command of the Union force reported:

Lieutenant, the expedition ordered out to recapture, if possible, the Government stocks stolen by guerrillas left this place July 12, 1864, with eighty infantry and twenty mounted men. They traveled in the direction of Sparta, Tenn., fifty-two miles, where they took to the right, so as to get into the head of England Cove, at which place the stock were reported to be. Just one mile this side of where they turned to the right, the advance guard was fired upon by one rebel, who made his appearance in the road before them. The guard returned the fire and the rebel fled into the woods. The command moved on till 10 p.m., and halted for the night upon the top of the mountain. At daylight the next morning they descended the mountains and reached the head of the cove, through which the Calfkiller River runs. On reaching that spot they again came upon the bushwhackers and fired some fifty rounds at them, which created quite an excitement in the valley, and all the men fled to the mountains. It was ascertained then that the stock had been divided among the captors and had been driven into different parts of the mountains and counties. however, some few of the stock were found in out-of-the-way places. The citizens would not give any information about the stock nor against the guerrillas and denied of knowing than any had been brought into that valley. The major commanding found that the citizens were all aiders and abettors to the thieving band. So he commenced to show them the rewards given to such people, and had their stock (private) and everything that his command could consume seized, and plundered every house from there to Sparta, finding in all thirty-three guns, some ammunition, and many articles which could not have been obtained except by theft, and destroyed all that could not be brought away. For a distance of fifteen miles down the valley every house where good stock, arms, or goods of a contraband nature could be found, the most unparalleled plunder was committed.[35]

"Unparalled plunder" may have created more guerrillas than it discouraged. The effect of such a policy on the civilian population was however dramatic. The results of such actions in the countryside were well summarized by a Union officer stationed at nearby McMinnville:

> I am also satisfied that in the present famine-like condition of the poor classes, many of whom would otherwise remain quiet and peaceable will, under the continual pressure of want of the necessaries of life, engage in robbery and every other crime, unless restrained or overawed by troops; neither would there be any safety for the lives and property of several Union families here.[36]

This was not the kind of war for which Alpheus Williams had enlisted. He was looking forward to joining the forces assembling at Chattanooga under William Sherman, but he did not anticipate an easy campaign:

> I expect to have a hard summer. The mountainous country in front is so poorly supplied for man or beast and we shall be so far away from supplies that I prepare for a season of deprivation. I really fear more for my horses than myself. We shall probably break up here next week and move to the front. When the fighting campaigning will begin I cannot guess.[37]

There was only a brief hiatus after Williams departed before the next commander of Sub-District #1 arrived and brought with him a policy of "hard war." Major General Robert Huston Milroy bore a grudge against all individuals associated with slavery and equally, a grudge against West Point-educated officers, who he thought conspired against him to deny his rightful chances to put down the rebellion.

Milroy was born in Washington County, Indiana, on June 11, 1816.[38] At that time Indiana was still a frontier society, and opportunities for education were scarce. Milroy never overcame his lack of a thorough education in his boyhood, despite attending college and becoming a lawyer. At age 24 Milroy left home and, using money he had saved from working at various jobs and in the family business, he enrolled at Norwich Military University in Vermont. It had long been a dream of Milroy to attend West Point, but his father refused to help him make the political contacts necessary to gain an appointment. Norwich Military University was chosen as a substitute for West Point because of its reputation as a good state military academy. Graduating at Norwich, Milroy tried to get a commission in the army but failed. He was convinced that West Point graduates conspired to keep those who did not share the same military education out of the service, and this was the source of a lifelong bitter distrust of professional military men.[39] Milroy found a chance to put his desire for military service into action when the war with Mexico broke out in 1845 and he raised a company of volunteers. He felt that he was prevented from winning a reputation as a soldier because his commanding officer in the First Indiana, a professional military man, was incompetent.[40]

At age 33 Milroy married Mary Jane Armitage. In time they would become the parents of seven children, four of whom died before reaching adulthood. In order to support himself Milroy had returned to Indiana to read law and to attend the developing state university at Bloomington. In 1854 he moved to Rensselaer with his growing family. Soon he was established as a lawyer there and became an elder in the Presbyterian Church. His heart was never in the practice of law, however, and he focused much of his attention on controversial matters. This probably hampered his law practice and damaged his reputation because he was called up before his fellow elders in the church for an investigation on two occasions. The first time Milroy had openly questioned church doctrine and on the second he had served as a second in a duel, for which the church suspended him from participation in church government.[41] At some point Milroy became an ardent abolitionist and welcomed the coming of war in 1861. "I saw the present war approaching and I watched it coming eagerly. I saw that my country could only get rid of the awful curse of slavery by a terrible bloody struggle. That our cup of iniquity was full and that God's justice could slumber no longer."[42] The war would also give Milroy an opportunity to realize his military ambitions.

Milroy began raising a regiment even before the first shots were fired at Fort Sumter, and consequently was able to report to Indiana Governor John Morton with the first complete regiment formed by that state. Since Indiana had sent eight regiments to the Mexican War, it numbered its first Civil War regiment the 9th Indiana. Milroy and this unit were assigned to the mountainous area of western Virginia, which would later become the state of West Virginia, and saw service under General George McClellan and General William Rosecrans. Milroy benefited from the success these men achieved in some skirmishes and, as a reward for his role, was promoted to brigadier general on February 2, 1862.[43]

In the spring of 1862 Milroy found himself facing General Thomas "Stonewall" Jackson as the Valley Campaign began. Milroy and his men spent so much time chasing and being chased by Jackson that they named themselves "Milroy's Weary Boys." Milroy's combat experience against Jackson at the battle of McDowell on May 8 and at the battle of Cross Keys on June 7 demonstrated the rather limited scope of the Hoosier general's military ability.[44]

When the major fighting shifted to the Peninsula of Virginia in June, Milroy remained in the mountains to help hold the backwater through which the important Baltimore and Ohio (B&O) Railroad passed. Although the railroad was an important Union supply line the area was a military backwater. In this setting Milroy found himself beset by small units of Confederate cavalry and numerous guerrillas. In an attempt to drive these units out of his area of command, Milroy resorted to a policy of retaliation. Whenever the property of Union citizens was taken for use by Confederate troops, Milroy made a levy on the pro-Confederate citizens equal to the value of the property taken. In enforcing this policy much property was burned and many civilians were shot. This policy of holding civilians responsible for the acts of military units was new to America and caused a considerable outcry. President Jefferson Davis asked Robert E. Lee to open correspondence with Union army chief Henry Halleck to have Milroy desist from this policy. Halleck, feeling that Milroy was beyond the pale of currently accepted military practice, agreed to do so.[45]

Instead of obeying Halleck's order to stop his practices, Milroy appealed to friends in the media and wrote newspaper articles justifying his actions. These articles appeared during the great battle summer of 1862 when it seemed that the Confederacy was well on its way to winning its independence. Many people in the North were not favorably impressed by the efforts of their own government to protect the lives and property of rebels and in the end, public opinion made it impossible for Halleck to enforce his order. Halleck never forgave Milroy this breach of military protocol. The Confederate authorities responded by declaring Milroy an outlaw, not entitled to protection by the rules of war if captured, but liable to be hanged as a common criminal. A reward was offered by the government in Richmond of $100,000 while the Virginia state authorities added $25,000 should Milroy be delivered to them, dead or alive.[46] These practices had become much more accepted by all Union commanders by the time Milroy arrived in Tennessee, but he was still an outsider so far as the fraternity of West Point men was concerned.

The road from Virginia to Tullahoma began at Winchester, Virginia, June 13–15, 1863. Milroy had about 7,000 men in the Winchester fortifications with another 1,800 at Berryville, 10 miles away. If these forces were properly used, Milroy had a chance to delay the Army of Northern Virginia on its march north and perhaps enable the Army of the Potomac to oppose Lee's crossing of the Potomac. The Confederate advance was led by Richard S. Ewell, recently promoted to corps command following the death of Stonewall Jackson at Chancellorsville. Ewell's management of his command at Winchester produced one of the best fought small engagements on the part of any Confederate force during the entire war. Ewell both flanked the town to the rear and successfully attacked the high ground to the west of town, routing the Union forces. Ewell captured over four thousand of Milroy's men, 23 cannon, three hundred horses, and a huge amount of commissary, quartermaster, and medical stores. Milroy personally escaped the debacle but was soon removed from command and placed under arrest by General Halleck, although charges and specifications were not brought against him.

For the next several months Milroy bombarded Halleck and Lincoln with letters asking for a chance to defend himself. Finally, a Court of Inquiry was called and Milroy had a chance to argue his case. Since there had been no orders to evacuate Winchester, there was no question of disobedience, only incompetence.[47] Milroy still did not have a command, but for political reasons Lincoln did not want to dismiss him from the army. After 10 months of idleness in Indiana, Milroy was tapped for the job of commanding the Defenses of the N&C RR, Military Sub-District #1. The commander of the Department of the Cumberland was Lovell Rousseau, who maintained his headquarters in Nashville. Milroy was of equal rank with Rousseau and would be 75 miles distant from his commander. These factors would give Milroy a good deal of leeway in the running of his command.

The command was not what Milroy hoped for. Milroy knew that this was a rear area, reserved for those who had failed to prove themselves in combat, but he did not see himself as a failure. He felt all his problems were the result of professional jealousy on the part of the West Point graduates and that their influence was such that even Lincoln had let him down. In letters written to his wife, Milroy never ceased to vent his anger at Halleck and the other professional soldiers who had assigned him a less than glorious role in the war. Milroy always felt his moral stance on abolition clearly marked him as a man who should be in combat command. He arrived in Tullahoma with a heart full of bitterness against his own superior officers, an offended sense of dignity and worth, and a well established record of harsh treatment for any civilians or irregular soldiers who dared challenge his control. Milroy was a shattered man seeking some shreds of military accomplishments with which to rebuild his life. "The dream of my life has been wrecked and destroyed by the grossest, most cruel, brutal injustice, for over 2 years my prospects were brilliant. I felt I was living to some purpose, that I was doing glorious service for my country and the cause of human freedom . . . The Bright Dream of my boyhood years and of manhood prime has ended in bitter disappointment, and I have a painful proof of the injustice and disappointment of man."[48]

On his arrival in Middle Tennessee, Milroy had under his command the 133rd, 134th, 135th, 136th, and 138th Indiana. These were all "100 Day" regiments, designated as such because of the length of their enlistment. Generally weak in training and discipline these units contained a sprinkling of veterans who had served a full term of enlistment in other units and then reenlisted for another, shorter stint of duty. Some of these regiments were still recruiting and others had been detained in Kentucky to guard against a cavalry raid. In organizing these troops, Milroy would have as subordinates Brigadier General Horatio Van Cleve, who would be in command at Murfreesboro; Brigadier Eleazer A. Paine, who would command at Tullahoma; and Brigadier Wladimir Krzyzanowski who would command the garrison at Bridgeport, Alabama. Similar to Milroy all these had once had combat commands and now found themselves relegated to a rear area.

For scouting purposes Milroy was assigned a brigade of cavalry composed of the 5th, 10th, and 12th Tennessee (U.S.) and two companies of the 2nd Kentucky (U.S.). This cavalry would remain with Milroy for most of his assignment in Tullahoma, but overall his command could be characterized as a shifting one, with units leaving as their short terms of enlistment expired and as other units came to take their places. On occasion Milroy received veteran units which had been sent to the rear to serve out the last days of their enlistment or who had suffered so many casualties that they had lost combat efficiency. Among these veteran units would be the 13th New York Artillery and the 59th Ohio. In February 1865, Milroy added to his ranks the 42nd Missouri, a unit which would appear frequently in the provost marshal records as practicing a "hard war" policy against guerrillas.[49]

The most active guerrilla leader at the time of Milroy's arrival was Robert Buchanan Blackwell, usually called Captain Bob Blackwell. There is no listing in *Tennesseans in the Civil War* for Robert B. Blackwell, so it may well be that Captain Bob was a true guerrilla, not enrolled in the Confederate army but motivated only by a desire to protect his home territory from the worst of war, and on occasion, to gain revenge. Blackwell was born on January 17, 1829, to Shrewsbury and Martha Gibson Blackwell. The family lived in several locations in Middle Tennessee, including Marshall, Lincoln, and Bedford Counties, areas where Blackwell later operated as a guerrilla. In the late 1840s the family moved to Texas for a time but returned to Tennessee. On July 23, 1854, Blackwell married Mary Jane Bagget, and the couple moved to the Richmond community in Bedford County. While living there, Blackwell first became constable, and later sheriff of the county. It is uncertain when he became a guerrilla, but by January 1864, Blackwell was already well known. The *Official Records* tell us that one of Blackwell's supporters

Captain Mosely, a guerrilla captain, escaped from custody on the evening of the 19th of January, under, as near as I

can ascertain, the following circumstances: For some reason unknown to me Captain Mosely was allowed to go
the house of Mrs. Blackwell, the wife of Captain Blackwell,
the guerrilla chief, accompanied by a single guard, to stay
all night. The guard went to bed and, of course, to sleep,
when Captain Mosely took a revolver from under his head,
and the horse of a lady friend of Mrs. Blackwell, conve-
niently near, and made off. Several messages have been
reported as coming from Captain Mosely since his escape,
of an unpleasant nature. During Captain Mosely's stay
here he was allowed to a great extent the freedom of the
place, and to receive any of his friends or sympathizers
who chose to call on him; was never sent to the guardhouse or turned over to the command of the post, but, on
the contrary, rather treated as a guest, who was entitled
to a guard of honor.

Taking into consideration this man's desperate character, the amount of trouble he has given the United States
authorities, the atrocities of every description committed
by him and his men (of which murder was probably the
most merciful) upon peaceful citizens, I thought it best to
lay before you some of the facts, so that if possible an investigation might be ordered, and the party or parties responsible for his escape brought to punishment.

While this Mosely was a prisoner here (or guest, as
you chose to term it) he had every opportunity to find out
the strength of the forces at this post, as well as their position, and any other knowledge that might be valuable to
an enemy. He was captured by Captain Beardsley's command and was in his charge when he escaped.[50]

This escape was soon followed by a "visit" from Blackwell's
guerrillas. Perhaps it was on the basis of Mosely's information, or, maybe, there was another system of smuggling information out of the town, but on the 13th of May Blackwell and
some thirty men rode onto the public square in Shelbyville

and spent two hours in calmly cleaning out the Brown & Harris dry goods store. Some of the contents of the store were soon being sent south to the Confederate forces. There were Union troops in Shelbyville and many more only seven miles away along an operating rail line at Wartrace, but Blackwell ignored these men to carry out his daring raid.

This bold action caused the Union army to take a particular interest in Blackwell, so a spy was sent into his camp. This encampment was located in the very area where the incident had occurred with the 9th Ohio Battery and the foraging train ambushed by Tolley's guerrillas. The spy reported to the commander of the garrison of the earthwork that guarded the railroad bridge across the Duck River in the vicinity of Normandy on May 22, 1864.

> Captain: I have the honor to report to you that I have ascertained from a Federal scout named Young that the guerrilla band or organization or bushwhackers that has infested this part of Tennessee for some weeks past now rendezvous near the head of Mulberry Creek, about fifteen miles nearly south from Shelbyville, and is composed of the following commands: Captain Davis, seventy men; Blackwell, seventy men; Blackwell now ranks as major; Roddy, sixty men; Roddy now ranks as colonel or lieutenant-colonel; Cruzer, forty men; — — — —, forty men — this name is forgotten — making in all 280 men. Cruzer seems to be operating along the line of Lincoln and Marshall Counties. The squad from Short Mountain, under Major Hughes, was at Fairfield on the 20th instant. Lieut Thomas Beattie and twenty men returned from a scout, on which he visited Shelbyville and Richmond; from Richmond he proceeded to within five miles of Lynchburg, thence to the head waters of Flat Creek, thence down said creek to Flat Creek store. Davis and Blackwell have been scouring that country almost constantly for the last three weeks. He learned that their headquarters was on Mulberry

Creek, near Mulberry village. The greatest number of men
of Blackwell's command seen together at one time in that
neighborhood was thirty-six. I learn that General Paine
will send an expedition through that country, if deemed
necessary, whenever you are ready.

I have the honor to be, Captain, your most Obt Servt
R.B. Stephenson, Major 31st Wisc. Vols [51]

When it was said that Blackwell was "scouring" areas of
Bedford County, the provost marshal records describe what
sorts of activities were occurring. Mrs. Martha Brown gave a
sworn statement in which she said she lived about 12 miles
from Shelbyville near the village of Richmond in Bedford
County, Tennessee. In late December 1863, one of her neighbors, Dr. Isaac S. Davidson, had come to her house and asked
to speak with her privately. Dr. Davidson had then warned
her that he had received reliable information that Blackwell
intended to attack the Brown's house in order to kill her husband and to take their horses. Since Mr. Brown had gone to
Shelbyville on business, his wife secured the help of a neighbor to ride along the Shelbyville road until she met her husband and warned him not to come home for several days.

Dr. Davidson also requested that Mrs. Brown tell no one
where she had gotten the information about the impending
attack. The doctor was convinced that if Blackwell learned that
he was warning people of planned raids he would be killed
and his property would be destroyed. The Browns had good
reason to fear Blackwell, having already suffered at his hands.
Their son, a member of the 5th Tennessee Cavalry (U.S.), had
been killed by Blackwell's men.[52]

The mixture of warfare and revenge is apparent in Martha
Brown's depositon. Her son had been killed while in the Union
service, albeit in a Union regiment which had a reputation for
plundering Confederate residents. Then Isaiah Blackwell had
been killed by Union soldiers, so Captain Bob Blackwell
planned a raid to seize the property of Union supporters and

to kill the most prominent known Unionist in the area. Blow and counterblow would become a standard pattern. Thomas J. Ladd was almost a victim of that pattern on the same occasion recounted by Mrs. Brown.

Ladd gave testimony that he was a Union soldier and that he had gone to the village of Richmond to attend the wedding of a friend. During the night before the wedding, December 30, 1863, Blackwell made an attack on the house where Ladd was sleeping. Ladd managed to escape but lost his horse and all of his clothes except the shirt and drawers in which he was sleeping. Wandering about the countryside in the freezing night he arrived half-frozen at the house of Dr. Isaac Davidson. Dr. Davidson welcomed Ladd, gave him a hot bath, dressed him in some of his own clothes, and instructed him on how to go across country to the home of another Union soldier named Gray Hyde. Again, as he had done with Martha Brown, Davidson warned Ladd not to mention his name in connection with the escape out of fear that Blackwell would kill him.[53]

The attention paid to "stock" was not only because animals were valuable and represented a substantial part of the wealth of any family, but because the guerrillas depended on good horses for rapid movement, which was the key to their safety. Just two days before the raid on Shelbyville, Blackwell went on a foray to get horses. He raided the farm of J. M. Hix, a Union supporter.

June 11, 1864

General Paine

Sir. I send you a description of horses taken from me recently by the thieves and robbers of our land. On the 11th of May at night there was a band of five armed men came to my house demanded entrance, three of them rushed in abused us and my family striking me on the head with their pistol. Shooting through the door shutter where my wife and children was, and passing through her leg & scraping my sons leg; they took from me horses of the following description; one beautiful dark dappled bay stallion five years old this spring 16 hands high hind feet white to the pastern; a small white spot over the right nostril; short weepainted ear, naturally paces on frontals all the time. One three year old stallion about 15 hands high blood Bay; no white spot; some white hairs over his right jaw; and opposite thigh gray appearance.

Ten days before Blackwell took the horses Hix described another group of five guerrillas had stolen a young mare from him. Because a heavy rain had left the ground muddy, the mare had been tracked by Hix and some neighbors for several miles to a hollow near Lynchburg, Tennessee. There the trackers came upon the camp of Blackwell and one of his allies, John Tolley. The trackers were promised they would not be harmed if they returned home and said nothing to the Union authorities about the camp.

According to Mr. Hix, some of the participants in the Shelbyville raid were James Whitfield, John F. Tolley, Button Tolley, Mark Parks, William P. Haslet, James Whitman, William Beavers, Robert Long, and other men whose Christian names were not known but whose surnames included Clark, Knuckles, Schotten, Rainey, Poe, Dousenberry, and Edens. Most of these names were well known in Bedford County and were all from families known to have Confederate sympathies. Blackwell had been in command of the force and was assisted by Captain Bill Davis.[54]

Not surprisingly, the raid had a rather depressing effect on business, so much so that one person who had come seeking financial opportunity now decided that opportunity was to be found elsewhere:

Shelbyville Tenn May __ 64

Dear Garner

You must not think hard of me for not writing to you more often but you know these are war times and we must be very careful. This town is full of Secesh and

Bushwhackers and it wont do for A Union man to express himself too freely. We have the 2d Kentucky here commanding and they are a fine set of men. The Rebels came in here a few days ago and taken off all the dry goods and clothing in town. The troops in command here have captured three or four horse thieves and I hope they will receive their just reward in the shape of a bullet. I am in business now but not making much money just as soon as I get a certain amount of money I am coming up there and then me and you will start a bar of our own. This country dont suit me and I am going to leave it. Sure give my love to Lizzie and the children and write soon.

Yours Truly

James Perkins[55]

This dissatisfaction was not confined to the Shelbyville business community. A man known in the provost records only as K.D., an informer and spy utilized by several Union commanders, vented his ire in a report to General E. A. Paine. K.D. was certain that nothing was going to be done about the goods taken from the Brown & Harris store at Shelbyville during the raid. The local Union judge advocate, Major Squires, had found evidence that goods in various private houses had been taken from the merchants, but no official in Shelbyville was willing to take action on the matter. Perhaps the Union officials feared the guerrillas. At any rate, K.D. urged General Rousseau to take action from Nashville before the goods could be moved beyond Union lines. K.D. was certain that Blackwell had the goods in his hands and that he was moving them south along a route which ran from Hurricane Springs to Hurricane Creek, then along Chestnut Ridge, and across country to a point six miles north and west of Tullahoma. From there they were dispersed. Another informer, T. W. Gordon, was certain that some of the goods had been "deposited with the wife of the notorious freebooter and thief R. Blackwell." He was certain that at least two wagon loads of goods had already reached Confederate-controlled territory.[56]

On June 15, 1864, Paine's command rode into the village of Fayetteville, the county seat of Lincoln County which adjoins Bedford County to the south. The morning quiet of the little town was shattered as troops came pouring into town, shooting left and right. Soon smoke was rising from numerous points as barns and outbuildings were set afire. Squeals of pigs and squawks of chickens blended with screams of terrified women as hostages were seized and dragged to the court house in the middle of the village. Four of the hostages were selected to be executed if no one came forward with information about Blackwell and the other guerrillas operating in the area. There was no evidence that any of the hostages were members of the guerrilla unit. All of them had been quietly going about legitimate business when they had been seized by Paine. One of the four, Thomas Massey, had been arrested as he came out of a store where he had purchased groceries for his wife and young children. William Pickett was another hostage seized because he was wearing a coat that had a Confederate army button, although the rest of the garment was made of civilian cloth. Franklin Burroughs had just left the courthouse and had in his pocket his wedding license for his nuptials the next day. The fourth victim was Dr. J. W. Miller.

As the hostages awaited their fate, John R. Massey rode into town. Word had reached him on his farm that his brother had been arrested and he had come to plead for his life. Going up to General Paine, John said, "My brother is innocent of any involvement in this war. He has never supported or fed a guerrilla. He has a wife and a young family. If you want Massey blood, take mine." Paine immediately accepted the offer and Thomas left town.[57] The son of one of the hostages recalled, years later, the events of the day:

> My father, Dr. J. W. Miller, was captured at the fall of
> Fort Donelson, carried to, and kept a prisoner of war at

Camp Chase for many months, at which place hemorrhage of the lungs became so excessive he was liberated and allowed to go home, but no provision was made for his transportation, nor effort given to assist him in any way, but being free and stimulated with the thought of going home, he set out afoot from Ohio to come to Fayetteville, Tennessee.

Following the public highways he would occasionally overtake someone, or a driver would overtake him, giving assistance, facilitating his progress. Many times he was arrested by some Yankee officer or private while within the Federal lines, but being armed with a "pass" he was just as often released.

Finally reaching Nashville, he was given transportation to Shelbyville, the Old Winchester and Alabama railroad having been torn up from Decherd to Fayetteville, he found friends at Shelbyville who assisted him in reaching home.

The Yankees, sometimes having possession of Fayetteville, followed in turn with its recapture by the Confederates, such proceedings being alternated occasionally, necessarily kept Lincoln County, as well as others adjoining in a constant state of uneasiness.

It so happened when my father returned General Paine had possession of town. A more merciless, cruel tyrant never existed than that damnable officer.

At the time John Massey, Pickett and others were arrested my father was taken in charge also. These men were not held together, all placed in charge of one guard, but were scattered.

The killing of these men occurred in the spring time. My father lived on Bridge Street at the top of the hill going down towards the stone bridge, adjoining the Davidson school house, opposite the McEwin residence.

The day of the arrest was a bright, sunny day. All nature was clad in its new garment of green. New Irish potatoes, English peas were about ready for the table and our first "mess" appeared then. My brother and myself had helped our mother get these vegetables from the garden, she having apprised my father of the fact that "We are going to have Irish potatoes and new peas for dinner." This delighted him as he was very fond of such things. Their pleasure and anticipation was soon swept away, followed by despair, distress, mental anguish, and vanishing hope—my father was arrested, charged with "harboring bushwhackers" the same as Massey and others.

The officers took him in charge at once, immediately carrying him away, giving my mother no information as to his fate, despite her pleadings for some knowledge of it, any more than to say "All damned bushwhacker harborers would be shot and sent to hell."

Her screams, her cries, her pleadings, her prayers are yet fresh in the writer's mind.

Upon the orders of Gen. Paine houses were burned here and there over the town; gunshots were frequently heard in different directions; anarchy reigned; consternation was everywhere. No one knew from hour to hour what would happen next. Minutes lengthened into hours.

My father was arrested about 10:30 and taken off. At 11:30 Mother received notice that all the prisoners taken, charged as just mentioned, would be killed at the same time. Gen. Payne had started towards Shelbyville with a large body, but stopped at or near the Gordon place for dinner.

The negro cook had proceeded with the preparation of dinner, despite all the confusion, and when Mother learned the soldiers had stopped for dinner, immediately prepared a meal for my father, sending myself and a little negro nurse to find and give it to him, if possible.

We found him sitting under a beech tree, surrounded by six or eight men as a guard. Upon delivering the dinner he courteously invited the guard to eat with him. They refused in a nice, sympathetic way, but admonished him to hurry as orders might be issued any moment to move.

While eating, Gen. Paine rode up, surrounded with his staff, all on fine horses, bright uniforms, sabers dangling. These officers wore gloves with large, yellow gauntlets.

Paine rode very near to my father, possibly not more than six feet away and enunciated his ever memorable statement (to me) saying 'You G-d d—m grey-eyed bushwhacking sympathizer, I'll have you shot at three o'clock this evening with John Massey and the other damn scoundrels.' This not only frightened me but the negro girl as well, who screamed, 'don't kill Marse Bill, don't kill Marse Bill.'

I grabbed my father by the neck, begging for his life, the negro doing the same thing at the same time. The officers of the guard forced us away and told us to leave.

When my father hugged me to his bosom, saying, 'Good bye, my little boy, I'll never see you again.' no one but a confiding child in similar condition can realize the awful agony of that moment.

No attempt will be made to tell the anguish of my Mother when the news was given her that 'Pa will be shot at three o'clock.' Not only my mother but the screams, cries, and wailings of others were heard everywhere.

My father was carried nine or ten miles toward Shelbyville, released, and stepped in home about sundown. Can anyone imagine a more joyous returning. He never knew why he was liberated and the others shot.[58]

The other three men were not so fortunate. They were executed at the spot where the Lincoln County Public Library now stands. It is said that as the firing squad formed up, Pickett and Boroughs fell to their knees to pray. Thomas Massey picked each of them up by their shirt collars and said, "Pray standing. Don't let these dogs think you are kneeling to them."[59]

Brigadier Eleazer A. Paine was well experienced in rough warfare before coming to Fayetteville. He had graduated from West Point in 1839 but had resigned from the army in 1840 to practice law. He had lived in Ohio and later in Illinois where he was elected to the State House of Representatives in 1853 and 1854. Paine had commanded troops at Cairo, Illinois, and had seen combat at New Madrid, at Island #10, and at the Siege of Corinth before he was assigned to railroad protection. He had earned a reputation early in the war as a "hanging general" when, following the death of one of his men, he issued orders to "Hang one of the rebel cavalry for each Union man murdered, and after this two for each. Continue to scout, capture, and kill."[60] For almost two years Paine had been in command of the Union garrison at Gallatin, Tennessee, and had created a perfect reign of terror while in that post. He had made it a regular practice to have prisoners killed without trial, and to order executions of civilians on mere suspicion.[61] Paine was a natural target for revenge by Blackwell.

On September 24, 1864, Robert Blackwell was moving through an area on the Tennessee-Alabama line known as Banyan Swamp. This was not a swamp in the usual sense, but was an area of flatland with numerous slow-moving streams which frequently overflowed in wet weather, leaving the whole area unfit for agriculture except for occasional hillocks and slight ridges. The swamp made an excellent route north and south for spies, couriers, and guerrillas since it was covered mostly in dense woods. As he travelled through the swamp, Blackwell was accompanied by Joe Kelly. Both men were wearing Union uniforms. About three miles east of Toney, Alabama, Blackwell passed near the farm of Mrs. Sullivan. This resident was a strong rebel and often fed and housed men passing through the area. At the time Josh and Tom Kelly of the 4th Alabama Cavalry (Captain Frank Gurley's regiment) were staying with her. These two saw Blackwell and Joe Kelly passing near the cabin. Since Blackwell and his companion were wearing blue uniforms they decided to capture or kill the two.

As they crossed the swamp to get in front of the travelers, they lay in ambush but recognized Blackwell before opening fire. The two parties then joined forces and continued north. Before they had reached Fayetteville they had met seven other guerrillas and had formed a plan to revenge the attack on their home base.

Using information which may have been obtained from female sympathizers in Shelbyville, the men approached the town on September 26. They made their plans to attack the railroad depot on the night of the 27th while they hid in the homes of Confederate sympathizers. They knew there were 21 Union soldiers in the building, but they believed that surprise would be to their benefit. As soon as the men in the depot were asleep, the 11 guerrillas surrounded the building and charged from all sides at once. Blackwell and Tom Kelly entered through the freight doors shouting, "Surrender, d—m you, or die!" The surprised Union soldiers surrendered and were soon on their horses, beginning the 23-mile ride to Fayetteville. As they rode out of Shelbyville flames leapt from the depot where the military supplies had been set afire.

As the men rode though the night Blackwell and Josh Kelly began to discuss what to do with the prisoners. Upon arriving in the village of Fayetteville the two men reached a compromise. Blackwell agreed to allow Josh Kelly to parole the "more respectable" prisoners, but the rest would remain in Blackwell's care. Kelly wrote out paroles for 11 men, which allowed them to begin the long walk back to Shelbyville. The other 10 were taken south of Fayetteville to the top of Wells Hill where they were shot. Local residents found their bodies the next morning. A note containing the words "Remember Massey" was pinned to each of the bodies.[62] Each of those who had been executed were Tennesseans who had joined the Union army, some of them after having been in Confederate service. One of their widows later testified:

> I live on Flat Creek Bedford County. My husband belonged to Wortham Co Home Guards. He was mustered

as a U.S. troop. He with twenty six others of the company was stationed at Shelbyville on the 28th of last month, when he with the other twenty-six of the company was captured by Blackwell's Co of Bushwhackers, who took the 26 to Wells Hill, where my husband with nine others of his company was shot by the bushwhackers. My husbands name was Berryman Bruton. I understand he lived two days after he was shot staying at the house of a citizen named Lamberson; and when he died was buried at Patricks Grave yard.

He was not in the Rebel Army.

I am satisfied that the families of Mr Samuel Broadway and David Wise used their influence to have him shot. They had threatened to have them shot before.[63]

Upon hearing about the raid and the subsequent killings Milroy was furious. Soon after he received the news, Milroy telegraphed his superior officer, George Thomas:

Ten of the home guards captured at Shelbyville by Blackwell were taken out and shot in cold blood. This was unprovoked and should be followed by a terrible retribution. Blackwell's wife lives in Shelbyville. I would recommend that she with the secesh women of the place be sent through the lines and his house burned, and that I be given an adequate cavalry force and about ten days time among the guerrillas of Lincoln County.[64]

Guerrillas were elusive and dangerous, and women, such as Blackwell's wife, were a much easier and safer target. Milroy's idea was fleshed out two days later by the receipt of a report from the mysterious K.D.

A LIST OF THE DISLOYAL LADIES OF SHELBYVILLE
                              Tullahoma Tenn Oct 14/64
Maj Genl Milroy

Sir, the government of the United States of America should know and understand its enemies whether male or female. And treason should be made odious in both alike, I am not making war upon "innocent" women; every brave man loves and respects the name of woman, but when she stoops from the high position that beautifies the character of a true woman and seeks alike, with traitors of the male gender, to undermine and sweep away the best government on earth she forfeits her claim to that high regard and becomes the most corrupt and debased of the whole human family. I repeat that I love the very name of woman, but when she unsexes herself she is a fit subject for anything. It is to them, in great measure, that this country, so beautifully adapted to higher scenes and more noble purposes is made one vast scene of carnage and blood. And have they repented? No! They are doubly distilled in their phanaticism. And shall they remain here among the people they so much despise to annoy the loyal people and give information to traitors? We cannot believe it just and we are aware that it is your purpose to reward patriotism and punish treason. These rebel women express a desire to go south or for the return of the gents of their complexion, and surely they should at least have one portion of their wish granted them, the portion that leads their minds and carcasses southward. Who says no? Not he that is tinctured with loyalty. The following is a list of applicants for a journey south and by all means they should not be disappointed in their lofty expectation. MRS WALLACE of Shelbyville whose husband is a refugee from justice now in the south. She is a most notorious rebel and has sold off all her furniture & etc and is trying to sell her place to go south. Her daughter and son John rejoiced greatly when Blackwell made his raid in Shelbyville. And I think surely Miss Cunningham and her mother merits a passport from a letter she wrote which by the way fell into your hands. Her brother is in the rebel army and his father is in the south. Nor would I forget to mention the daughters of Robt Matthews who hugged and kissed the rebel Genl Robinson when he and Williams came through Shelbyville and rejoiced when Genl Robinson told them that he was the man who killed Co. Eiford of the 2nd Ky. Their father is in the south and claims that he was the first man who proposed to break up the Charleston Convention in 1860. Blackwell's wife should also be sent south for her health. There is also a Mrs Fuqua (wife of John Fuqua) who prays that blessings may once more fall upon the rebels. She should be at last allowed to "risk one eye" and her husband should be allowed the same privilege. Miss Felicial Whitthorn and her sister, Mrs Thomas, (whose husband is in the south) both shed many tears because they can not get to go to the promised land. They merit a glance. And I must not forget Mrs Mary Wooten whose husband is in the South. She wished the earth might open and swallow up the Union army and all of the Union people and also that Blackwell might catch and hang every Union man who was lying out from home. Lee Dalton, Baley Blessing, E.M. Patterson and Pattersons wife saw four rebels ride up to Mrs Wootons house during Forrests raid and talk with her half an hour and when they left they went immediately to get the news and she swore that she had seen no one. She sends letters and gets letters from the rebel army almost every week.

Who merits a trip south more than Mary Wooton? She is a splendid spy for the rebels and should be sent south. Next comes a Mr Watson (whose given name I do not know) and his wife and daughters who reported John A. Moore and his son Moses Moore to Bragg while he was at Murfreesboro for borrowing green back money, to aid his son A.G. Moore in escaping north to prevent the conscription and said John A. Moore a peaceable old man 64 years of age and his son Moses Moore 16 years of age were arrested and sent to Murfreesboro and imprisoned and badly treated for many days. They should not have the honor of living one moment more among loyal people. And justice to humanity and the interest of government requires that they be sent to Brownlow's next Depot to the infernal regions. Other names could be mentioned but time will not admit.

I am respectfully, K.D.[65]

The proposal to deport Mrs. Blackwell met with some unexpected opposition in the form of a letter of support for Mrs. Blackwell.

Shelbyville Nov 26th 1864

Major Genl Milroy, Commanding—Tullahoma
Dear Sir

We the undersigned loyal citizens of Bedford County understand that Mrs Blackwell, wife of R.B. Blackwell, has been ordered South. We respectfully ask that the order issued by you to go be revoked, for the reason that she disapproves of his conduct. She has written him advising him to abandon his command and return home, take the oath, and become a good citizen. At this he took offense at her and when he was in here, the time of the Wheeler raid, he went to his home & only spoke to his children & not to her. This caused her to turn [three words illegible] she could, the conditions of Union people. Numerous facts of which they have been unfounded and which they claim true.

Under the circumstances & for the reasons aforesaid, we hope the order will be revoked unless she desires to go South. My information is that she does not. The application is not made on account of Blackwell, but for the lady.

J. H. Baker   C. H. Bean
Wilborn Limbaugh   A. C. Grant[66]

Milroy was not deterred by the opinions of these Union supporters and on the same day that this request was sent to

Milroy, Mrs. Blackwell and two children departed on their way south, moving rapidly and with little baggage. Their arrival was noted at Dalton, Georgia. "Mrs Mary A. Blackwell & children, the wife of Captain Blackwell of Forrest's Command, was received from Tullahoma, November 25, 1864. To be sent through U.S. lines South. Recd the above from K.W. Mansfield Capt 12th Michigan Vol I & Pro Ma."[67]

It is not known where Mrs. Blackwell and her family found refuge during the remainder of the war, nor how they made their living. The stress on the relationship between Mrs. Blackwell and her husband must have been intense, if the testimony of the "Loyal Citizens" is to be believed. The family is known to have returned briefly to Shelbyville following the war before moving to Texas. Robert Blackwell was killed in Texas in mysterious circumstances. A dispute arose with a neighbor over a dog, and Blackwell spanked the neighbor's child during the argument. The next morning Blackwell was shot from ambush by persons who were never identified.

In November 1864, Milroy had not heard the last of Robert Blackwell. He and his command continued to be present and active in the area for the rest of the war. At times it was clear that Blackwell was following the "black flag" of murder and revenge more than he was serving any other banner. His actions, and the retaliations taken by Federal forces, made human life a very cheap commodity in Military Sub-District #1.

> Maj Genl Milroy
>
> I send to you under guard William J. Donaldson of Bedford County with the following charges—that he the said William J. Donaldson was present in association with Blackwell and seamed to be pointing out the men when Blackwell was separating them to be murdered he also fell in with Blackwell and traveled some fifteen miles— he also had on his person when arrested a number of applications used by the Local agent of the county for the purpose of shipping goods from Nashville to this

prospect—an exact copy of those used at his office—he also had the reputation of being a noted thief.

Respectfully, your Obedient Servt

James Wortham Capt & Pro

Witnesses

E. Lockard, Sergt   Ed. Cunninham Pvt   W.L. Lacey Pvt

B. Wright, Pvt   Virgil Jones Pvt   4 Tenn Mounted Inf.[68]

Some of the guerrillas in that band were better armed than most of the Union troops trying to control them. One such guerrilla was Issac D. Dowdy who was armed with a Spencer rifle and two revolvers when he was captured near Shelbyville. Dowdy had earlier taken the Oath of Allegiance to the United States and had a copy of the oath on his person when captured. Apprehended with him was his brother, D. J. Dowdy, a deserter from the Union army who had been charged with stealing horses. "They are both very bad men," said Major John Worthan in closing his report of the capture.[69]

Some of the guerrilla activity was not orchestrated by organized bands at all but reflected the term "bushwhacking" in its truest sense as disgruntled citizens took up arms to resist the Union forces. On at least one occasion these men acted with more courage than good sense.

Jacob Molder, a Union soldier from Bedford County, Tennessee, killed by bushwhackers during the winter to 1863–64

Author's Collection

Major Cravens, Sir—

I ordered the arrest yesterday of A.J. Troxler and G.M. Courtner of Bedford Co. Tenn living in the vicinity of Duck

River Bridge on the N&C RR—suspected of being concerned in the shooting of a Picket of the 31st Wis Vol at
Duck River Bridge on the night of June 3d 1864. I examined them this morning and elicited the following facts.

A.J. Troxler examined—says he lives 1 mile South of
Duck River Bridge—has taken the oath of Allegiance to
the U.S.—says he was conscripted in the Fall of 1862 into
Newman's (Rebel) Batt—was on duty at Shelbyville and
Winchester. At the time of Bragg's retreat from
Murfreesboro he obtained a Furlough and returned home
and says he has remained there ever since. On the night
the picket was shot, Troxler states that himself and family
went to bed between sundown and dark and that none of
his family was up during the night, but the Pickets say
there was a light in his house immediately after the shot
was fired (say 11 P.M.)

G.M. Courtner examined—he claims to be a farmer—
was arrested early in the fall of 1862 charged with burning R.R. Bridge over the Duck River and at time took the
Oath of Allegiance to U.S., but while under guard broke
away and was shot by the guard and was severely
wounded. After his recovery he volunteered in a Rebel
company being formed in his neighborhood but states he
was exempted by the Conscript Agent (Rebel). Courtner
denied in the commencement of the examination that he
had been in the Rebel Army but afterwards admitted the
fact of his having volunteered in a Rebel Company with
his certificate of having taken the Oath of Allegiance to
the U.S. in his pocket. One double barreled shot gun was
found in Courtner's possession in the morning after the
Picket was shot, one barrel of which had evidently been
discharged. A U.S. Springfield musket was also found in
the house of said Courtner's father, living inside the guard
line at Duck River. The citizens in the neighborhood of
Duck River Station state that Troxler and Courtner are both

unmitigated and dangerous and bad men. I ordered the prisoners back to the Stockade to await your orders.[70]

This guerrilla activity greatly strained the resources of the pro-Union citizens of the area since the guerrillas took their horses and goods for use in the military efforts against the Union army. Reflecting on his Virginia experience, Milroy sought to make the rebels pay in the most literal sense. He proposed "that I be permitted to make an assessment on the rebel sympathizers in the vicinity of the locality where the losses occurred to reimburse the Union men named above for the losses sustained." Among the Union men Milroy wanted to reimburse were Dr. Crank, who had lost horses, grain, and other property amounting to $1,500; Patrick FitzWilliam, who had lost furniture and provisions worth $639; Parson Wells, who had lost two horses, corn, and provisions valued at $550; R. J. Churchman, who had lost undisclosed property worth $27; Samuel Charles, who had had his horses and mules taken by the guerrillas and who was owed $670; and M. Hix, who had lost horses worth $250.[71]

Threats and reprisals did not deter the guerrillas, as they continued to swarm around the railroad. On one occasion, a party of irregulars led by a man named Grant cut the telegraph between Decherd and Cowan nine times in one night. They also tore up some track and lay in ambush for the work party which came to repair their damage.[72] On another occasion they struck at the top of the Cumberland Mountains in a fashion reminiscent of an Indian attack on a frontier stockade.

> Hdqrs. Detachment Second Massachusetts Infantry
> Sir: I have the honor to submit to you the following report of the expedition sent by your order under my command to Tracy City on the evening of the 20th instant.
> The expedition consisted of details from the Third Maryland, Fifth Connecticut, and Second Massachusetts (in all about 100 men and one commissioned officer, Lieutenant Clary, Third Maryland), under myself, proceeded

about 8 p.m. up the railroad some 6 miles till we neared
the water-tank on the Tracy City Railroad, where we found
a train awaiting us. The men were immediately put upon
the car, and we proceeded toward Tracy City till within
about 4 miles of the town, when we slackened the speed
of the train. When within three-fourths of a mile from the
trestle bridge which crossed Gizzard Creek, about a mile
from the town, and which is somewhat over 150 feet long,
the men were disembarked and skirmishers thrown out
about 60 paces in advance of the main body, and the command was cautiously advanced toward the bridge. Having leaned from the inhabitants of a cottage near by that
no firing had been heard and no enemy seen in that vicinity, and that our pickets were posted on the farther side of
the bridge, I left a corporal and 10 men in an unoccupied
stockade, near the southern end of the bridge, and proceeded across, but found no pickets on the other side. True
we were in fear that the enemy had captured them, as
well as the troops in the town. I then proceeded cautiously,
keeping the skirmishers well advanced, till we reached a
small trestle bridge about 300 yards from Tracy City depot, where I halted and sent 10 men across to ascertain
who were in possession of the town, and by whom was
the stockade occupied. These men soon returned, reporting that the town and stockade were in our possession;
and I thereupon advanced into the town and occupied
the stockade, in which latter I found about 40 men and a
lieutenant of the 20th Connecticut Infantry, it was then
about 1 a.m. I found on investigation, that about 3 p.m. a
body of guerrillas, about 100 in number, had made a dash
into the town, coming in from two opposite directions so
suddenly as completely to surprise the pickets and out-
posts. The captain (Upton) of the 20th Connecticut commanding, who was within the depot at the time, having
with him about 15 unarmed men, immediately started for

the stockade (about 200 years distant) but being cut off before reaching it was shot, after throwing down his revolver in token of surrender, and taken prisoner, together with about 15 of his men. Close to the stockade was a log building occupied as a store by a certain Benham. The rebels made a dash for this, and shot 1 of the men of the 20th Connecticut who was standing in the door-way, seriously wounding him. The store-keeper, who was within, immediately closed the door and fired with his revolver upon them from the window, wounding 2 of the band.

Upon this they returned toward the railroad, thus giving our men an opportunity to enter the stockade, which they then immediately occupied under the command of Lieutenant Jepson, of the 20th Connecticut. The enemy then, after deploying along the edge of the woods surrounding the town, sent in under flags of truce four separate summons to surrender, which being refused, they proceeded to set fire to the depot, engine-house, and some buildings connected with the coal works. They paroled and set at liberty 10 of their prisoners. Of the remaining nothing has been heard. A man named Kennedy who owns a house in the place, and who was arrested several nights before on suspicion of being a spy, but who effected his escape, is supposed to have guided the rebel party into the town. I remained with my command in the town till 8 a.m. of the 21st, when, seeing no signs of the enemy in the vicinity, and in accordance with your orders, I embarked my command on board the cars and returned to Cowan, where I arrived at 12m.

I have the honor to be, sir, very respectfully, your obedient servant

Jno F. George, Captain Co. E, 2nd Massachusetts Inf.[73]

Under the lash of such constant tormenting attacks, the patience of the occupation troops began to wear thin. When a guerrilla was caught, he often received short shrift and rough justice. LaFayette Swanner, of Lincoln County, Tennessee, was one such case. Even though he had taken the Oath of Allegiance, he was accused of acting as a conscript officer for the Confederacy, of stealing $20 in cash, and some dry goods, and a horse from Joseph Webb, a Union Man, all on the same day. Several of Webb's neighbors gave testimony against Swanner. One of them was James H. Harrelson, who said:

> I have known him [Swanner] for the last 10 years he joined the 32 Tenn C.A. he was captured at Fort Donalson and sent to Indianapolis to Camp Morton I saw him again about two years ago he was then Bushwhacking. About the month of Sept he came with 7 or 8 men to where I was at work and stole two horses belonging to me . . . he was at the house of James Kirkpatrick when they arrested him for being a Union man I with others went to rescue Kilpatrick and . . . we killed two of their party and arrested LaFayette Swanner when a council was held and as there was no Union Military post we were afraid to do anything with him and let him go.[74]

In additional testimony, another neighbor, David M. Tafts, swore that he had gone with Swanner to Fayetteville to take the Oath of Allegiance on July 28, 1863. The next winter, in February 1864, Swanner had gone to Taft's house with a gang of bushwhackers and robbed him of a pair of pants. The same gang had returned the following May and stole money and jewelry. James J. McCann swore that Swanner had entered his still house and taken horses and harnesses from him and from several of his neighbors.[75] Swanner was found guilty and was sent to Tullahoma to be placed in the stockade. A laconic entry in the provost records on March 23, 1865, affixes a firm ending to the story of LaFayette Swanner:

> A.W. Billings, Major & Pro Marshal
> I have the honor to report to you that LaFayette S. Swanner a prisoner while in my charge going from Fayetteville to

Tullahoma attempted to escape and was shot dead by the Guard.

    G.B. Johnson 2 Lieut Co D 5 Tenn, Comdg Guard[76]

During the time that the guerrillas and the occupation forces faced each other, the location of the larger war had shifted. In early September 1864, Sherman captured Atlanta. His Confederate opponent, John Bell Hood, who had replaced Joseph Johnston, had moved back into North Georgia and succeeded in luring Sherman out of Atlanta. Sherman's original orders had been to destroy the opposing Confederate forces, and capturing Atlanta was to occur as an end result. Because the capture of Atlanta occurred without the destruction of the Confederate forces, the Army of Tennessee was free to dodge about the mountains of northern Georgia and Alabama. No longer hampered by defending what had once been its supply base and a vital rail junction, the Confederate forces were in a position to attempt to deny Sherman's men the fruits of their victory at Atlanta.

Sherman learned two lessons in October of 1864: he was not going to trap the Army of Tennessee, and his armies could subsist off the countryside. As a result of these lessons Sherman turned toward the sea. Confederate General John Hood decided to ignore Sherman's move and attempt to recapture Middle Tennessee. Sherman sent General George Thomas to organize a defense for Tennessee and ordered General James Schofield to reinforce him. South of Military Sub-District #1, across the Tennessee River, shrouded by the heights of Sand Mountain, thousands of Johnnie Rebs were marching toward Tennessee. Nashville, even Murfreesboro, were securely in Union hands but all the little posts along the railroad were at risk. A sharp watch needed to be maintained to avoid being surprised by the rebel cavalry and also to be sure that they could withdraw to safety in time when the main army came their way. The "big war" was returning to Tennessee.

3

The Unknown Final Frenzy

Franklin and Nashville are two battles synonymous with blood. The "last hurrah" of the Confederacy in the West ended in blood and gore, to say nothing of courage and fortitude, in December 1864. As the contemporary wags sang, to the tune of "The Yellow Rose of Texas," "the gallant Hood of Texas played hell in Tennessee." To most people it was obvious that the war was over, the Confederacy had lost, and spring would bring its final collapse. Histories of this period of the war typically gloss over the closing months of the conflict with only a sketch of the last battles around Petersburg, the final Confederate offensive in North Carolina at Bentonville, and then the drama of Appamattox and Durham Station.

But to those in Military Sub-District #1, Defenses of the N&C Railroad, the winds of war did not blow softly to a close; a better characterization would be one of a final hurricane. The guerrillas seemed to be determined to have one more drink of blood; the Yankees were set on extracting the ultimate pound of flesh before peace came. Instead of quietly winding down, the war behind the lines entered a final frenzy, which has remained unknown until now.

In November 1864 Tullahoma was the largest Union garrison for 50 miles in any direction. The presence of the Northern forces there encouraged numerous Freedmen, or former slaves, to throw up rough shelters around the village, and in many cases, to obtain employment in the Quartermaster Department. The Freedmen had evacuated the village when the Yankees left. Milroy noted that "It was painful to witness the terror, excitement, and anxiety among the negroes when it became known to them this place was to be abandoned by our troops. Many hundreds had congregated here, mostly women and children, who had left their Rebel masters and were living in hundreds of little cabins built in and around town. The men having gone off in our army either as soldiers, servants, or teamsters."[1] Upon returning to Tullahoma in December 1864, Milroy found that the guerrillas had wreaked havoc during his absence. The cabins of the Freedmen had been destroyed, left-behind military supplies had been taken, the post sutler's store had been ransacked, and pro-Union civilians experienced the revenge of their Confederate neighbors. Milroy immediately swung into action by interviewing "loyal" residents to determine the extent of their loss. The owner of the sutler's store, D. P. Rathbone, reported personal as well as business losses:

> In accordance with your request I herewith hand you a list of articles and merchandise taken from my residence by the Bushwhackers and Citizens belonging to me and my firm of Lasater and Rathbone during the recent evacuation of the Union forces of Tullahoma. No estimated value of the same is such as the articles would sell for in this market and much of it, the sum that the articles actually cost.
>
> I was absent from home at the time, consequently know but little of the parties. Mrs Rathbone was at home at the time many of the articles were taken. She represents the men as being disguised and made every exertion to keep from being known. I am credibly informed that one James Randal, son of David Randal, living 5 miles N.E. of Manchester was implicated in the matter.

But most particularly two young men by the name of − −
Rogers and − − living in − − [These blanks appear in
the original]

I am well satisfied that most of the robbing was done
by men belonging to the Guerrillas under Hays. I am not
personally acquainted with him and but few of the men
belonging to said band. And give you the name of such as
I know.

John F. Ross and I.G. Rodes live 8 miles North of
Manchester near the Manchester and McMinnville RR.
Wiley I Hines, lives 6 miles East of Manchester and Randall
who I have spoken of.

I would respectfully refer you to Mr E.A. Call and W.T.
Hart well known at Head Quarters for further information of parties belonging to Hays Guerrillas.[2]

In a later report Rathbone added details of the damage
that the vengeful guerrillas inflicted on his property. He reported to Major A. W. Billings, the provost marshal in
Tullahoma, that

On my return home I found that the house had been
broken open, the shelving had been chopped down & most
of it carried away, the counters much chopped and
haggled up.

Our iron safe sustained the greatest injury. We left the
outside door open and unintentionally left the inside vault
locked. This was broken open, the door being broken in
two pieces and lock mined — the partitions (made of ma-
hogany wood) were all chopped out and nothing is known
of them.

On learning these facts I was quite indignant and remarked that I would like to know the one that perpetrated
this act. When Mr James P. Edwards (artist of this place)
remarked that he could tell me, as he saw what was done.
And then stated that when Furguson was in the house he

(Furguson) took a hatchet in hand, knocking down the
shelving & chipping generally, and he bade him to cease.
I don't remember the reply that he said Furguson made.
For further particulars I would most respectfully refer you
to Mr. Edwards and Mr Jo B. Smith they were here, and
endeavored to protect the property & saw much that was
going on.

D.P. Rathbone[3]

Those who were genuinely innocent, or who feared the
consequences of receiving missing and stolen goods, turned
themselves in as was the case with William Norvall, a tanner.
During the period of the Union evacuation, guerrillas brought
19 cowhides to his tanyard and "insisted" he purchase them.
Since the hides still had the initials "U.S." branded on them,
Norvall knew they were government property. With the return of the Union garrison, the tanner was anxious not to be
found in possession of stolen government property, so he contacted the provost and requested that the hides be taken away.[4]
Since leather goods were such valuable commodities it may
be questioned whether or not Norvall had truly objected to
buying the hides from the guerrillas. His hope may have been
to have time enough to process the hides and resell them before a return of the U.S. forces.

Some men, like Joel Smith, were truly innocent of wrongdoing in possessing government goods, as was proven by testimony by Union soldiers. Lieutenant Abe Pelham of the 3rd
Michigan Infantry gave a sworn statement to the provost that
as he was leaving Tullahoma during the evacuation he gave to
Joel Smith seven sacks of oats from the forage the U.S. troops
were being forced to leave behind. The lieutenant made a plea
that Smith not be held guilty of any wrongdoing for having
the remains of the oats on hand.[5]

Milroy still felt that Confederate sympathizers should pay
for the losses of their Union neighbors. He had pursued that
policy in Virginia early during the war and as a result had

gotten in trouble. Now because public opinion had changed, such retaliation was thought to be in order. The local pro-Union citizens submitted lists illustrating amazing quantities of goods and their estimated value that had been taken by the guerrillas. These lists reflect the social and economic climate since they typify the contents of an average household at that time. Although the lists are quite extensive, one example serves to make the point:

> Lists of articles taken from citizens during the evacuation of that place by the Federal Forces from the 30th of Nov to the 21st of Dec 1864 by bushwhackers and disloyal citizens.
>
> The following are the list of articles robbed from Mrs Mary A. Norton.

8 Yards of Jeans @ $3.00 per yard	$24.00
12 yards white linsey @ $2.00 per yard	24.00
9 yards Blue mixed cloth @ $1.50 per yard	13.50
11 yards Extra fine cloth (black & red) @ $3.00	33.00
30 Brown Muslin $1.25 per yard	37.00
1 Bed Blanket	10.00
4 Silver Spoons @ $5.00 each	20.00
4 Silver Forks @ $1.00	4.00
2 Pair Ladies Shoes @ $4.50 each	9.00
1 Ladies belt	1.00
1 Pair mens Socks	1.00
$6.00 in money	6.00
Other articles too numerous to mention	17.00
Total amount in money	$200.00

> Asa Grant, Joseph Rogers, James Rogers, — — Rhoton, Kinsey Cobb and a man named — — are the persons who robbed her.

> List of articles robbed from Moses Pittman by Bushwhackers who were invited to do so by Robert Smith and Jane Lipscum

4 horses	$800.00

1 rifle	40.00
1 double barreled shot gun	30.00
1 Colt's repeater	40.00
1 Bowie knife	10.00
75 Barrels shelled corn	375.00
600 pounds pork	75.00
1 three year old heifer	25.00
Total amount in money	$1395.00

RECAPITULATION

Mrs Mary Ann Norton	$200.00
Mr Burn's Daughters	95.00
Mrs Lehr	60.00
Mrs Malvina Potter	107.00
John T. Thomas	25.00
D.P. Rathbone	389.00
Lasater & Rathbone	230.00
M. Shoffner & Co	880.00
William Shoffner	1520.00
W. Fletcher Byrom	127.00
Mrs Brinton	165.00
Matthew T. Cunningham	410.00
Moses Pittman	1395.00
Total Amount	$5605.45[6]

Milroy's intention was to assess pro-Confederates in the area to compensate for the losses of the Union supporters. To aid him in this effort he had the most determined soldiers he would command throughout the entire war, the 42nd Missouri Infantry, mounted, and under the command of Colonel Forbes. The unit reported to Milroy on January 2, 1865, after having learned the trade of guerrilla fighting on the Missouri borders.[7] A few weeks after their arrival in the Tullahoma area, a Confederate who had given himself up and had signed a parole, commented on the 42nd Missouri. "I remarked to the citizens that I was taking with, 'I have seen a great many Yankees, but there goes the hardest looking gang that I ever saw.'"[8]

Milroy apparently made a careful financial analysis of the ability of several citizens to pay reparations and also assessed the degree of pro-Confederate sentiment held by these individuals. It was not considered necessary to prove anyone guilty of a specific charge. If General Milroy felt a person was pro-Confederate, that was proof enough. Soon targets for retribution had been selected from local Confederate sympathizers. A list of names was prepared by the provost and beside each name was the amount of money Milroy thought that person was able to pay. The first list was titled "The following named citizens are disloyal, and can be assessed for damages done by their Bushwhacking friends for the amount set opposite their names and are perfectly able to pay it" and contains 42 names and lists a total of $3,040 to be paid. A subsequent list itemizes the names of people who were thought to be harboring two guerrilla leaders, Poe and Grant. The eight names on this list have $215 in assessments levied against them. Another list names 18 individuals living in the same neighborhood and "harboring Hays and his gang of Bushwhackers" and they are fined $1,400. Then came names who "live in the same neighborhood and harbor Easton and Green's gang of bushwhackers" and who are fined $825. At the end of the document is a heading saying, "The following persons live within a small circle of ten miles of each other and are bitter 'Secesh' and can well afford to pay a small subscription in lieu of damages done by their Bushwhacking friends" and giving nine names who are assessed $200. In all, Milroy declared that the "Total sum that can be collected from all the above named persons in the above neighborhoods is $8280.00." The "Total amount of losses handed in up to date at the HdQrs by loyal citizens is $5603.45. The Balance remaining is $2676.55."[9] A total of 68 names appears on the list. Since the amount collected is greater than the damages claimed here is another example of money collected with no record made of its disbursement. As General Alpheus Williams had noted in an earlier quote, some people grew rich off the misery of war.

Milroy was not entirely satisfied by paying back the Union population for their losses. Partly out of a sense of justice and partly out of a desire to humiliate those on the other side, the general decided to replace the housing of the Freedmen who had congregated around the village and whose shelters had been destroyed during the Union evacuation. The commanding officer of the 42nd Missouri received the following orders:

> During the temporary evacuation of this place lately by the U.S. Forces under the Maj Gen Cmdg the Guerrillas came into town and robbed peaceable citizens of loyal character and behaved in a most shameful and cowardly manner more resembling savages than persons professing to be civilized. They were particularly severe upon the Negroes who were left in the place and took particular pains to burn every Negro cabin house and shanty in town.
>
> Therefore as an example and a warning in future to that class of robbers and murderers and as a simple act of justice to a helpless and inoffensive class of people who are unable to help themselves and the fruits of whose labor for a whole Summer and Fall have been swept away in a most wanton manner it is the intention of the Maj Genl Comdg to make the relatives friends and the aiders abettors and advisers of those who committed the act repair the damage which their bushwhacking relatives and friends here committed.
>
> You are therefore ordered to bring thence up from the country a list of whom is hereto appended (marked "A") and compel to build up every house owned or occupied by Negroes that were destroyed and place in as good if not better condition than they were before.
>
> Also the list that is attached marked ("B") will be required to furnish subsistence and anything that may be necessary for the comfort of their friends in this list of those marked "A" while they complete the job.

Any other details not mentioned within which may
be necessary to complete the work are left to your discre-
tion. And a guide will be furnished you upon application
to point out the residences of the persons who are within
this lists.

Fifty-four names appear on the "List of citizens who are
to work rebuilding burned Negro shanties," while 30 names
are on the "List of those who are to furnish rations tools &
etc."[10] Many of the people on both of these lists had previously
been listed as fined by Milroy to repay the losses of "loyal"
citizens.

At the time that Milroy was giving the orders to rebuild
the houses of the Negro refugees in Tullahoma a temporary
flurry of excitement ensued as a major Confederate cavalry
force passed nearby. For several weeks General Hylan B. Lyon
had been leading rebel cavalry on a rampage in Kentucky. He
had attacked Cadiz, Hopkinsville, Princeton, Madisonville,
Hartford, Campbellsville, and Burkesville in the Blue Grass
State before finding the odds so great that he advised a with-
drawal from Kentucky. On January 7, 1865, General Lyon, with
seven hundred men and two guns, crossed between Decherd
and the Elk River, heading towards Salem, Tennessee, and the
Alabama line. Milroy had no cavalry to interfere with this escape since the 5th Tennessee had "straggled off home" or was
out on a scout.[11] But with the backs of Lyon's men in view,
Milroy decided to take more drastic action.

I started Lt. Col Stauber of the 42nd Mo V.I. with an
expedition of 300 men today to evangelize the country
between Elk and Tennessee Rivers in Guerrilla Missouri
style—that is by fire and blood. I have by experience become a firm believer in the doctrine that "There is no sal-
vation except by blood." There is nothing like it for the
poison of treason which brought on bushwhacking, robbing, murdering, thieving, etc. I find fire and blood properly administered to be the perfect balance.[12]

Just a few days later Milroy wrote:

> Started Lt. Col Stauber of the 42nd Missouri Infantry in command of an expedition to take Lincoln County and dress that county up for presentation to the Union. Lt. Col. Stauber had with him detachments of the 42nd Missouri and the 43rd Wisconsin and Captain Sparks' company of Independent Scouts from Alabama.[13]

There is no mention in the Provost Marshal's Records or the *Official Records* of the actions of these detachments, but given the facts which are recorded, imagination can furnish a vivid and accurate picture.

Milroy had an additional force to use against guerrillas; in conjunction with his occupation troops, he deployed Home Guards. The formation of such units had been authorized on September 14, 1863, by Major General Stephen A. Hurlbut, whose order covered Kentucky and Tennessee. Officers commanding divisions in those two states were authorized to create Home Guard units "from unquestionably loyal men" and were to organize them under the militia laws of their respective states. These "Home Guards" were not to be required to duty beyond the limits of their local area but would be expected to put down and repress robbery and irregular warfare within their area. They were to report all actions to their division commander. This organization was intended to function as an armed police force in which all officers and men of the unit were held responsible for their actions. They were to arrest and send forward those who had been arrested accompanied by a list of charges and names of witnesses. It would be the responsibility of the provost at the nearest military post to try and punish those who had been arrested by the Home Guards.[14]

Milroy worked hard to create a force to be reckoned with. He succeeded to a limited degree. To become a Home Guard officer, one needed testimonials illustrating one's loyalty to the United States. Men had to be recruited to serve, although they could be armed by the U.S. Army if they had no arms of their own. Several such companies were formed in Milroy's area of command, more than in any other part of the state of Tennessee. In each case the person nominated as an officer to head a Home Guard unit had to be endorsed by an individual known to Milroy to have strong pro-Union sympathies. One typical nomination is that of J. P. Weddington.

> Major, I have the honor to recommend the bearer Mr J.P. Weddington as a Loyal citizen and a high minded and honorable citizen. He has been elected Captain of a Home Guard Co and I would recommend that he be confirmed as such.
>
> E.A. Call[15]

Other Home Guard officers included W. L. Riggins of Normandy,[16] John C. Patterson of Fayetteville,[17] and F. M. Wright from near Fayetteville.[18]

Given the conditions which existed in the area, joining the Home Guard was not a step taken lightly. Those who joined quickly found themselves engaged in the risky business of combat.

> J.R. Shofner being duly sworn deposes and says:
> That in December 1864 five Bushwhackers, James Grant, Martin Poe, Ben Stanfield, Corpl Pless and one Rose being in the edge of Franklin County near Marble Hill village came to the residence of Thos Boyers in Bedford County for the purpose of having certain men who, the Home Guard Co of which I was a member had captured, rendered up to them. I was at Mr Boyers at the time with five others when they came up. They demanded that we should give the men up which we refused and opened fire on them with such weapons as we had. They retreated and we learned afterwards that Rose was wounded and I have learned from my brother since that he is now at his home still suffering from the effects of the wound.[19]

The Shasteen family had quite a different experience with Home Guard duty. William Shasteen was placed in charge of a Home Guard unit and paid the ultimate price.

Tullahoma Sept 14, 1864

Know all men by these presents that reposing confidence in the loyalty, honesty, and integrity of William Shesten of Franklin County Tennessee he is hereby authorized and empowered by these presents to enroll and command a company or squad of men or home guards scouts not to exceed twenty (20) in number to scout in the counties of Franklin, Lincoln, Bedford, and Coffee, for the protection of the loyal inhabitants of these Counties and for the purpose of driving and exterminating all guerrillas, bushwhackers, horse thieves, and armed rebels their aides and abettors and to capture all property belonging to such persons. The said William Shesten to be responsible for the conduct of the men of his company, and see that they do not rob, plunder and steal from Loyal citizens, and to be subject to orders from these Head Quarters. To report his doings to the Military Commander at this place, as often as twice a week if possible, and to continue the organization of said Company at the pleasure of these Head Quarters.

R.H. Milroy, Maj Genl Commanding

I hereby certify that I have repeatedly give orders to the two Capts Shesten to burn the houses of all persons who were known to voluntarily harbor and assist Guerrillas and Bushwhackers, and that in obedience to my orders they did burn and destroy a number of such houses.

R.H. Milroy[20]

Five months later Milroy had to issue another commission to another member of the Shasteen family, thus illustrating just how dangerous the business of serving in the Home Guard was.

Tullahoma Feb 14, 1865

This is to certify that William Shasteen the Captain of the within named company of Home Guards having died of a wound received from a company of Bushwhackers while in command of his company and in the discharge of his duty, and reposing the same confidence in the loyalty and integrity of his brother Elijah B. Shasteen within expressed in the said William deceased I hereby appoint the said Elijah Captain of said Company, subject to the same conditions, duties, and obligations as within imposed on said deceased.

R.H. Milroy, Maj Genl Commanding[21]

Elijah was a brave man to have replaced his brother under the circumstances, but he paid the same price.

Mrs Elizabeth Chasteen being duly sworn deposes and says I reside in Franklin County Tenn. On Saturday the sixth day of May AD 1865 at about 8 o'clock P.M. just as my husband (Elija Chasteen formerly a scout for Gen Milroy) had retired with myself and children we heard horses coming up the road. I remarked to my husband there are the Guerrillas after you. He answered yes and seizing his pistol and gun went up into the loft to shoot them as they entered the house but seeing so many sprang down and throwing open the door started to run. This occurred so rapidly that he had not time to put on his clothes but started out in his night dress. The last words he addressed to me being hide my clothes. As soon as he started to run the guerrillas exclaimed there the d____d rascal goes shoot him. I called to him to run but they the guerrillas says to me shut your d___d mouth or we will shoot you down. The last I saw of my husband he was running and the guerrillas were after him shooting at him incessantly. In half hour or less the guerrillas returned to my house and ordered me to open the door. I answered the doors open. They entered and ordered me to strike a light. I tried and failed told them they would have to strike the light themselves which they did and then commenced searching the house looking into every crack in the wall my bureau table and stand draws breaking open boxes and ripping up beds & c. They took every article of clothing my husband had. One of them, the guerrillas, put on my husbands coat and hat and boots. Stole all my jewelry my own and childrens clothing that they did not take off they threw on the floor and stomped under foot mostly or quite ruining it. They remarked to me when they returned to the house well old lady your husband ran well. I answerer I hope he has run well enough to get away from you. One of them says well we've killed him. I remarked well men if you have you have left me in a mighty bad fix. The answer was yes but it many a one left that way. I had no idea that they had killed my husband until the next morning when his body was brought back to the house. So destitute of clothing did they leave me that I had to send to get clothing to bury him in. I do not know how often or where he was wounded. When I saw him his head was thrown back and covered with blood. They took all my coffee and other groceries and one horse which they still have worth three hundred dollars ($300). Besides all his clothing they got his gun 2 saddles and any thing of value. I should think I sustained a loss of fully Six Hundred ($600) dollars if not more in property taken and destroyed. I failed in recognizing any of the guerrillas. Have no idea who they were. As we laid down that night he my husband placed his arms where he could get them at the same time remarking I do not believe the Guerrillas will ever come here. I answered you do not know and he scarcely laid down when they came. After the guerrillas returned and had killed him they asked me where Conner Awalt was. I said I did not know they remarked that he my husband had called him as he ran through the fields.

Elizabeth Chasteen X her mark[22]

A pattern of revenge and counterrevenge emerges from the provost records. Among those who had been killed by the Shasteen brothers were their neighbors, the same neighbors whose houses the Shasteens had burned. The foundation was being laid for a dysfunctional society once the war was over. There would be no peace among neighbors for years to come. Many people who went west after the war were trying to get away from feuds as well as to find new economic opportunities.

The Home Guards gave as well as took, inflicting casualties of their own on the Confederates. While Hood's Army was in Tennessee, many men and officers of the Confederate forces who wandered away from the main force while on visits home became victims of the Home Guard. One such event occurred in Shelbyville, a town with a considerable pro-Union population. Here, too, the hand of neighbor was turned against neighbor. The event was related by an eyewitness some years after the war:

> On December 6, 1864, it being a mild and pleasant winter day, Captain Thomas P. Mitchell accompanied by a fellow soldier came galloping into Shelbyville heading up the tree lined Shelbyville, Murfreesboro and Nashville Turnpike to the Whiteside mansion. Capt. Mitchell, who was only 30 years old had slipped into town behind enemy lines to see his wife [a daughter of the Whiteside family] and 9 month old daughter, Margaret, whom he had never seen. After about an hour's visit with his family, he and his companion mounted their horses and left to rejoin their unit. But in riding on the pike, they were discovered by a band of Home Guards form Wartrace who gave instant chase.
>
> At a fast gallop, Capt. Mitchell and his companion proceeded west, along the Fishing Ford Pike. About two miles outside of town they were overtaken by the Guards and, seeing no means of escape, they surrendered. The

Home Guards paid no attention to their surrender and continued firing, shooting Capt. Mitchell through the lungs. Falling from his horse, the Guards left him wounded and rode back to Shelbyville where they stopped at the Whiteside house and yelled out, "Hello."

Upon hearing the loud call at the front gate, Mrs. Mitchell ran to the front door only to hear one of the Guards yell out, "You had better send someone out to see about Mitchell. We shot him and left him for dead about two miles from town. You will find him out there in a fence corner."

Becoming alarmed, Mrs. Mitchell ran to inform her family who began collecting bandages, medicines and liniment and immediately proceeded to locate the body. On passing down the pike they hurriedly stopped at Dr. Thomas Lipscomb's house to have him ride out with the family, not knowing if they would find Capt. Mitchell dead or alive.

They found Capt. Mitchell's body where the guards said they had shot him and he was still alive but mortally wounded. The next day, Capt. Mitchell was carried back to the Whiteside house where he remained alive for only a few days, dying from his wound on Friday, December 9th.

At that time, there was a few Confederate scouts in the county, scouting behind enemy lines. Upon hearing of the death of Capt. Mitchell, they sent word to his wife they intended on giving him a military burial. Mrs. Mitchell made plans for her husband's interment for the following Sunday in Willow Mount Cemetery. At 4:00 on that bleak Sunday afternoon, Mrs. Mitchell with her grieving family surrounded the casket at the grave site in company with a few Confederate comrades. After scriptures were read from the Bible and taps were sounded in the distance, and the first shots were fired over the grave in

military honor, alarm was suddenly sounded that Yankees were fast approaching the cemetery. The family froze
in fear and at that moment a soldier jumped on his horse
and with full speed rode out of the cemetery where he
met head on with the enemy. It was the same Home
Guards who had killed Capt. Mitchell. A skirmish followed on the road outside the cemetery in which one of
the Yankees was killed.[23]

The deaths of Captain Shasteen and Captain Mitchell were
tragic and one can feel the pathos of the grieving wives, but
there is a darker side to the story. The Home Guard was more
than just a group of "Galvanized Yankees," they had used their
position to even old scores and to help themselves to the goods
of their neighbors. Despite the instructions not to rob, pillage,
or plunder, that is exactly some of the behavior that had been
undertaken by many of the Home Guard units.

Testimony to one occasion of robbery is contained in the
deposition of Pleasant A. Hoffer. On October 10, 1864, Hoffer
was at Tinsley's Wood Yard, five miles south of Tullahoma,
along the N&C tracks when a man named Perryman, a member of the Home Guard, robbed William Hart of two or three
pairs of shoes. Hart also told Hoffer that Perryman and another member of the Home Guard, whose name was unknown,
had taken two horses from other citizens in the same neighborhood. One of the horses, a sorrel mare, was offered for sale
to William Brandon who lived in Franklin County in the vicinity of the village of Hawkerville. Mr. Brandon had not
bought the mare, and Hoffer said he had seen Perryman riding
the mare just a few days past.[24] Authority to maintain the law
was readily converted into opportunity to break the law.

The same experience was reported in Warren County
where another Home Guard unit "took forcible possession of
one horse, one saddle, one sheepskin, and one violin" from
the home of Mr. A. Northcutt. The group then threatened to

kill Northcutt's elderly father if they did not receive some brandy.[25]

Another report of Home Guard misdeeds came from Franklin County and involved Elijah Shasteen. Shasteen had accompanied his unit to the home of Daniel Scivally in Lincoln County, where he had taken two mares, which horses were later seen in Tullahoma.[26] In Jackson County, Alabama, near Bridgeport, Captain Sparks of the Home Guard took horses from W. R. Waggoner, along with the saddles and bridles for the animals.[27] One farmer reported losing so much of his livestock to the Home Guard that he would not be able to make a crop in the coming spring.[28] Other citizens simply had their homes rifled by marauding bands of Home Guards. Andrew Swanner reported the Home Guards of Captain Lewis' command took $42.50 in money from him as well as clothes and household furnishings.[29] Yet another complaint came from a Matilda Swanner in an adjoining county that members of Captain Lee's Home Guard unit had taken her only mare.[30]

Youths were not exempt from Home Guard revenge, especially if they were captured by Calvin Brixey. Rough justice was given Captain Brixey at last, however, and with his many former misdeeds in mind, one wonders that it came so late.

> Hawkerville Franklin County
> This day personally appeared before me Jno P. Hindman of Coffee County and made oath as follows:
>
> During the past year of eighteen hundred sixty four I taught school within two hundred yards of Hawkersville. About the 1st of September, & about two o'clock p.m. Capt Brixey and Jim Kenniatzen came together to my school house. Capt Brixey appeared a good deal under the influence of spirits. Captain Brixey asked me the names of some of the larger boys and upon my mentioning the name of Jesse M. Abernathy, one of my pupils, he asked Jesse what right he had to confiscate his (Brixey's)

**Whiteside House where C.S. Captain Robert Mitchell
was pursued by his Union neighbors**

Captain Mitchell's grave

His funeral service was inter-
rupted by a skirmish with the
Union Home Guard.

brandy. Jesse answered that he had not done so, or if he had drank some of his brandy it was in ignorance of it being his — that the brandy was offered him by Dow Farris & he thought it was Dow's. Brixey then said Jesse should pay for the brandy & Jesse agreed to do so.

Brixey then said that he himself individually had command of this county — that the Rebels might, it was true, come the next day & send him galloping to Hell, but he'd be G— —d d— —d if he did not rule this county now, that Jesse Abernathy and his father were both G— —d D— —D Secesh, and if they did not leave the country it would be bad for them for he didn't intend any Secesh should live in this country. Captain Brixey then arrested Jesse and another boy and started with them to Decherd. About two hours later a Regiment of Rebel Cavalry came from towards Decherd with Captain Brixey as prisoner. Jesse M. Abernathy was an orderly, inoffensive & industrious pupil.

Captain Brixey was a drinking character & had the reputation of being a violent bloody man.

J.P. Hindman[31]

Captain Brixey's Union Home Guard had been a scourge to the area since 1863 upon the completion of the Tullahoma campaign. He was never seen again following his capture.

The wide range of country covered by these selected reports indicate that the Home Guard in general was out of control. The Union authorities concurred with this assessment after it was noted that "the home guard is responsible for almost all the nigger whippings which occur in the entire area," prompting the major general in command of the District of Middle Tennessee to take action.

General Orders No. 55
1. All home guard organizations in this District, unless organized under the authority of his Excellency, the Governor of the State are hereby disbanded.

By command of Bvt Maj Genl Johnson
W.B. Smith Major & AAAG[32]

However, some thought the Home Guard to play a necessary role.

Maj Gen Thomas
    Having received an information than an order was about to be issued disbanding he Home Guards in this county organized by the order of Mar Gen Milroy we the undersigned citizens of the County and members of Home Guard Companies beg to respectfully petition you in behalf of the further continuance of said organization, and to request that no order be issued at this time interfering therewith Coffee County 7th and part of 11 districts.
    Since the organization of this company our neighborhood has been remarkably quiet. Bushwhackers and Robbers have almost entirely disappeared and People feel a degree of security they have not felt before in three years. We therefore request that we be allowed to continue our organization until the militia of the State shall have been organized believing such a policy the best that can be pursued for our community at the present time.

One hundred forty seven names are signed to this petition.[33]

While the Home Guard did not consistently operate effectively, some of the measures taken by Milroy against the bushwhackers and guerrillas had at least some effect. On March 10, 1865, Major A. W. Billings, provost at Tullahoma, forwarded a list of prisoners including those guerrillas who had surrendered to Nashville. They included Nathan N. Wood, Lieutenant J. A. Hunt, J. A. Harper, G. A. Arnold, James S. Strong, John Arnold, Marion Rhoton, R. A. T. Stevenson, J. U. Hensley, Jesse Granstaff, and A. G. Martin. Others were merely listed as captured and included Joseph Russell, a "notorious guerrilla," James Odle, David Coppinger, R. L. Hoover, G. W. Lovelace, Logan Jacobs, Lieutenant J. A. Barnes, John S.

Renfrew, and Samuel Renfrew.[34] Those who were sent to Nashville would appear to be the fortunate ones. Milroy noted in his diary on February 10, 1865, "I have sentenced or rather ordered the notorious bushwhackers named Nance and Regan to be publicly hung today between 12 & 4 p.m. The scaffold was erected—the prisoners taken out & placed on the scaffold & they were making speeches, etc, when a telegram was recd by a man from Gen Rousseau ordering them to be tried by a military commission."[35] As this entry in the provost marshal records reveals, execution without trial had become commonplace in occupied Middle Tennessee.

Not content with capturing and defeating various bushwhacker gangs, Milroy still felt that the civilian base of support for such bands needed to be destroyed. He believed that his policy of "blood and fire" was the best way to accomplish such a task. Milroy found allies among those individuals who had been affected by Hood's return to Tennessee in November and December 1864.

Moses Pittman was one of the pro-Union men who had been attacked by guerrillas during the absence of Union troops from Tullahoma. His list of stolen and lost goods included several weapons, horses, and household goods. Pittman provided Milroy with a list of goods for which he was seeking restitution as well as a list of his neighbors who he felt deserved punishment for "disloyal" actions.

> Names of some disloyal citizens of the Fourth district Franklin County Tenn. A narration of their crimes and the orders of Maj. Genl Milroy as to what punishment they shall suffer for said crimes.

| Richard Arnold | A bushwhacker with Hays, he together with two others murdered a Loyal man named Samuel Kennedy in cold blood on Oct. 15, 1864. |

Horace Allred	Harbors bushwhackers and bushwhacks himself occasionally, is one of the murderers of Kennedy, is a shoemaker and makes shoes for all the bushwhackers in the neighborhood.
Bush	Nothing is known of the residence of this man or his first name and probable the name "Bush" is only a nickname. He is a bushwhacker.
Joel Cunningham	He is the leader of a gang of bushwhackers 75 to 100 strong. KILL [The notes calling for action appear in a different handwriting and are the orders of General Milroy as to the punishment to be received]
Wesley Davis	Harbors Bushwhackers. CLEAN OUT.
Green Denison	A bushwhacker with Hays. KILL
Jane Lipscum	A widow. Harbors bushwhackers. CLEAN OUT
Curtis McCullum	Harbors bushwhackers and instigated his son and three others to murder in cold blood a Union man named Samuel Kennedy on Oct 15, 1864. He has tried his best to persuade every young man of his acquaintance in the neighborhood to join the gang of bushwhackers. His wife is as bad if not worse than he is. has been doing all the devilment that he could ever since the war began. HANG AND BURN

Cynthia McCullum	Wife of the above and also instigated her son to murder Kennedy, the same remarks that apply to her husband apply also to her with double force. She is a very bad and a very dangerous woman. SHOOT IF YOU CAN MAKE IT LOOK AN ACCIDENT
Charlotte McCullum	An unmarried sister of the above and is almost as bad as her mother. BURN EVERYTHING.

The list goes on for a total of 58 names.[36]

Because of Pittman's list, Milroy issued orders to Captain William H. Lewis of Company A, 42nd Missouri Volunteers on January 7, 1865. The orders directed:

> Sir: You will proceed to the residences of the persons herein named and deal with them in accordance with the following instructions. In all cases where the residences of the persons are ordered to be destroyed you will observe the following previous to setting them on fire. You will first search their houses and premises to see if they have any articles belonging to the U.S. Govt or that are contraband of war, which you will bring away in case any are found. Also all or any of the following articles that may be found belonging to aforesaid persons.
>
> **First** All horses, hogs, sheep, cattle, and any other animals or articles of whatever description that may be valuable to the U.S. Govt especially those that are valuable to the Quartermaster, Commissary and Hospital Department.
>
> **Second** All stoves and stove pipes of whatever description and all kitchen utensils, Queens ware, beds, bedding, knives, forks & etc also all chairs, sofas,

Major General Robert H. Milroy, commander of Military Sub-District #1, 1864–65

Courtesy Library of Congress

Captain William H. Lewis, Company A, 42nd Missouri Volunteers

Lewis commanded one of Milroy's "death squads."

Author's Collection

sociable lounges and everything of the character of household furniture.

Third   All windows, sash, glass, looking glasses, carpets, & etc

Fourth   Every article of household furniture which you do not bring with you must be destroyed or burned with the house.

Fifth   All barns, stables, smoke houses, or any other outbuildings of any description whatsoever or any building or article that could possibly be of any benefit or comfort to Rebels or Bushwhackers their friends or any person aiding, abetting, or sympathizing with Rebels Bushwhackers & etc which could be used for subsistence for man or beast will be destroyed or burned.

Sixth   All animals forage or other articles brought in by you will be turned over to Lieut J.W. Raymond A AQm on this Staff to be subject to the order of Maj Genl Milroy to be disposed of as he may think proper, taking a receipt therefore from Lieut Raymond.

Seventh   The train accompanying will be subject to your orders, together with all the person connected with it, whether soldiers or civilians and you will cause any of them who may be guilty of committing depredations upon Loyal citizens or their property to be arrested and you will not yourself or suffer those under your Command to commit any trespass, or do any damage to Persons or property except those specified in this order.

Eighth   You will burn the houses of the following named persons, take any of the articles named above that they may have, together with all forage and grains belonging to them that you can bring away which may be useful to the U.S. govt for military purposes or otherwise and will give no receipt of any kind whatsoever. Joseph How, Dist. 11, 1/2 mile south of Hillsboro one mile west of the Hillsboro and Winchester road.

[There are a total of seven names in this section of the order.]

Ninth   The following persons will be shot in addition to suffering in the manner prescribed in paragraph # 8.

[Four names appear in this section of the order.]

By command of Maj Gen Milroy

Thos Worthington Lt 106 OVI ADC

On your return you will report in person to these Hd Qrs and give an account of what you have done.[37]

These orders were soon placed in action. Leroy Moore, Thomas Saunders, and William Saunders were three of the men that had been ordered to be executed in paragraph nine. Leroy Moore was described as "an old, white haired man" while Thomas Saunders was "over 50 years of age," and William Saunders was only 14. When the detail from the 42nd Missouri reached the Saunders house Moore was found to be visiting them. All three had their hands tied behind their backs and were forced to wade into a mill pond at Huffers Mill. They were then shot in the back and their corpses were guarded for three days before the families were allowed to remove them from the water. The method of their execution was the same as that styled "barbaric" by General Slocum and General Thomas when three of their men were murdered at Mulberry in 1863. The three are still buried on the banks of the mill pond.[38]

On February 7, 1865, nearly identical orders were issued again to Captain Lewis of the 42nd Missouri. This time 18 persons were listed under paragraph eight ordering their homes and goods to be burned. Thirty-four persons were ordered to be shot under paragraph nine, and an additional paragraph was added.

> **Tenth** The following persons have committed murder and if caught will be hung to the first tree in front of their door and be allowed to hang there for an indefinite period. You will assure yourself that they are dead before leaving them also if their residence they will be stripped of everything as per the above instructions and then burned.

[Four names are included in this section.]

If Willis Taylor is caught he will be turned over to Moses Pittman and he will be allowed to kill him.[39]

The instructions about hanging the men in their own door yard suggests that a hangman's noose was not to be used. Such a knot would cause death instantly, but these men were to be hanged with a simple slip knot so that they would slowly strangle. Before their departure the U.S. troops were assigned the task to yank on the legs of the hanged, breaking their necks, ensuring they were dead. When hanged in such a fashion death occurs after five to ten minutes of excruciating agony. The fury of war, as waged by the Union provost marshal, had reverted to torture methods of the Middle Ages.

Although Milroy sought to intimidate the guerrillas in order for them to leave his men and the pro-Union citizens of the area around the railroad alone, the guerrillas had the opposite goal in mind. They sought to intimidate the Union sympathizers and those who were neutral so that no information or aid would reach the U.S. forces. Because so much of the countryside was under guerrilla control, their task was easier and they, too, were capable of the most extreme forms of violence. The town of Winchester, Tennessee, would experience one such exhibition of violence in late 1864. The personal accounts from the provost records relate the story best:

Edward Butts (colored) being duly sworn deposes and says I reside at Winchester Franklin County Tenn. Am 29 years of age. I was born a slave and held as such up to June one year since when I left home. Since then I have been working for the United States Government.

On or about the first of November 1864 I was at Winchester. Had just gone home from work to see my wife. Just about daylight on the morning above named I came out of my house and started down the street. I saw some soldiers many of them having blue clothes and I supposed they were Federals until I saw a horse in the crowd which I had not seen with the 5th Tenn. I then turned my course and went to Brazelton Corner near where Huddleston (colored) lived. I there got over the fence behind a little shoe shop to hide from them. Two men came down the street to where I was, dismounted and came over the fence. When they come up to me I said good morning. One of them replied hello what the hell are you doing around here. When I replied Nothing they then asked me if I did not stay in that house last night. I told them I did not they replied yes you did I said no Sir I did not. One of them said to the other look there Sam and see if he stayed there I believe he is the G— —d D— —D S— —B— — we're looking for. Sam then looked in the house and replied no by G— —d nobody stays in there. They then told me they were looking for Bill Huddleston and they knew he stayed in one of these houses and I went round to the front door of the house of Bill Huddleston (colored) or where he lived, by this time the balance of the squad came up, one they called Captain rode up to me and said good morning. I replied good morning, he then inquired if there wasn't a man in that house there who had whisky. I said who, Bill Jones, he said no! Bill Huddleston was there living in this house. I said Yes Sir. He then told me to wake him up. I told him the door was locked and I could not get in, he replied rouse him, he's got to come, G— — D— —and burst the door down. I then stepped to the door, shook it, and called on Bill to get up he answered me, got up and came to the door, as he opened the door I whispered to him and told him they were Rebels as I said good morning to him the Captain said good morning Bill. He replied good morning Sir. The Capt then said step over here Bill, I want to see you a moment. Just as he stepped out to the edge of the pavement the Capt pulled out his pistol and presented it at his head and said walk out here Sir! He was slow about coming when the Capt said ain't you going to come out, he replied Yes Sir. The Capt said well get out G— — D— — right quick or I'll blow your brains out you G— — D— — S— —of a B— —. Bill said Yes Sir, let me get my shoes and pants and hat. The Capt then said G— — D— — you and your hat to hell get out here and that G— — D— — quick. Bill then went with him to the public square between the Court House and Brooks Company. The Capt then dismounted and was taking off his halter or working at it. The next thing I saw was Bill pulling off his shirt. I then shut his door and left and got off about two hundred yards when I heard the licks distinctly at that point. I stayed there for an hour and they were still whipping when I left. I did not know any of the men. Saw Huddleston at his house after he came back and found the skin whipped off him back neck shoulders and arms being perfectly raw and his eye shot out. I supposed one of the men to be Nance and afterwards felt confident that it was him from the fact that he said he was going to see his sister Mary and being called Sam Nance by the Capt after he had left.

Edward Butts X his mark[40]

The victim of the violence also testified under oath and said:

> I reside at Decherd Station, Franklin co Tenn. I am forty seven years of age. Was born a slave and held as such up

to the time the Federal forces occupied middle Tenn. As soon as the Federal forces came I went with Genl Davidson as servant. Have been connected with the Federal army all the time from the time I first went with Genl Davidson up to the present. have served in the capacity of guide for scouts.

Before the U.S. soldiers occupied this county I lived with my master at Winchester county seat of Franklin co Tenn where I had a wife and one child. On the first day of November A.D. 1864 I was at my wifes in the town of Winchester where I had gone from Decherd Station. Just after day light on the morning of the 1st of Nov 1864 I found my house surrounded by bushwhackers. One of them whom I know to be Sam Nance ordered a colored man named Ned Butts whom they had pressed to show them the room I lived in to get me out of there or break the door down. Said Butts (colored) said he could not get in when Nance replied G— —D d— —m him I know he is in there and we are going to have him. Ned Butts then rattled at the door. I then bid my wife and daughter fare-well saying I knew they were going to kill me. I then walked over and unbolted the door. One of the guerrillas said there he is Capt, G— —d d— —m him. Nance then says good morning to you. I replied good morning and he says I am going to kill you this morning. I replied all right Capt. He says what do you think about that you damn Yankee son of a b— —h. I replied all right Capt the bullet that kills me will save the life of a better man perhaps. Nance then says I am going to beat you to death you damn Yankee son of a b— —h. I says please Capt kill me where my wife and daughter can get my dead body. He says strip yourself god dam you I am going to beat you to death right here. The Chief of the command, one Hays then rode up with Nance says Maj here is the Comdr of the Post at Decherd the d— —d Yankee son of a b— —h. Maj Hays then got off his horse and said where is something to whip him with. One of the Guerrillas says take my saddle girt Capt. Maj Hays said all right have it off here. Hays took the saddle girt (a heavy cow hide girt) and split it so it had three lashes. He says boys keep a good watch out. I was to stand in a ring formed by the Guerrillas who were all armed. I was stripped to the waist my shirt lying in the street. Hays then fell to work on me administering seven hundred (700) lashes with the girt on my bare back. He whipped me until I could not stand alone. They then let me rest on my hands and knees for a few moments. I suppose Hays did the whipping because he was the largest and strongest man in the party. Maj Hays being about six feet three inches high and weighing about 180 pounds. After I had rested so for a short time Nance called Willis Taylor and four others whose names were called out but I cannot recollect them and ordered them to take me and forwarded me on. During the time they were whipping me there was no effort made by any of the citizens to stop it although there were quite a number on the street. When the Guerrillas started off I saw several women whose names were Miss Fanny Estel, Miss Poindexter, and a Mrs Frazill put biscuits and sweet cakes in the haversacks of the Guerrillas who were taking me off. They saying hurray for our men. Although they saw me and were perfectly cognizant of the horrible barbarity practiced on me. As soon as Nance ordered Willis Taylor and the four others before named to take me back Taylor said to me double quick you d— —d son of a b— —h. The Guerrillas were all finely mounted and I on foot. While towards the last of and after they had stopped beating me my back was burning as soon as I got warm my back became sore and very painful. I hobbled along the best I could. The guerrillas all the time urging me faster for about three miles and one half when Nance who had stopped in Winchester to see

his sister Miss Mary Nance and his Uncle and Aunt Mr &
Mrs Madison Porter came riding up and says the Yankees
are coming close up boys. Taylor says to me get faster you
damned son of a b— —h or I will blow our brains out. He
says if you make any step other than going as fast as you
can I will kill you right here. I answered Master I am doing he best I can please let me get up on your horse behind you. he says like h— —l I will. Nance then came up
again and says to them to the mountain boys and dispose
of him and then fall back to the road and if we have our
people wait and if we have come on to North Salem you
know where. Taylor and the 4 men took me and made for
the mountain about a mile and a half from where we had
started. When we reached the mountain he Taylor says
this is far enough. Then speaking to me he says now you
G— —d d— —d son of a b— —h if you have anything to
say say it now as you have two minutes to live. I asked
him if two minutes was all he answered yes by G— —d it
is. I then said well crack away when you get ready. I was
standing on the ground on the lower side of the hill and
he Taylor was sitting his horse on the upper side. As soon
as I said crack away he fired the ball striking me just
above the right corner of the right eye cutting the eye-
ball in two and forcing the ball out on the cheek where it
hung by the membranes surrounding it, the ball ranging
downward passing through the roof of my mouth destroying the palate and lodging just against the skin on
the left side so close to the jugular vein that it could not
be cut out where it now is. As soon as the pistol was
fired I fell forward and partially raised myself on the left
side but thinking they might fire again I fell forward as
though dead. One of the four then dismounted and struck
me on top of the head with the butt of his gun twice and
once atop the face. They then rode their horses on me as I
lay on the ground the corks of the horse shoes leaving

their imprint on my person which is still plainly visible. They then rode off and left me for dead. I suppose about that time I became unconscious. How long I remained in that state I do not know. When I came to I felt cold and chilly. I could not see at all, the blood from my wounds had clotted in my left eye so I could not open it. I had heavy whiskers and from the hair of my head to my whiskers was a mess of clotted blood so thick that when it was treated they had to cut off my whiskers there. I remember passing a flat rock which had a hollow in it filled with water and as I was suffering for the want of water began to crawl around hunting for it. After crawling round over the rocks and cliffs I found myself on level ground in wood I crawled on for some time when i heard men talking. Fearing they were Guerrillas I crawled under some brush or small growth and lay still until I could no longer distinguish voices. i then crawled off until I came to a fence. I pulled myself up by the fence and crawled into the field. I then straightened myself up by the fence trying to see if I could walk as soon as I turned loose of the fence I fell down again so I crawled through the field over and through the briars and into the woofs again. After I had crawled for some distance I hears someone chopping with a small ax or hatchet. Knowing that the guerrillas would not be chopping I called to them. They came a man by the name of Hilly Shores as I after ascertained. As soon as he came up I said if you please knock me in the head. He says Joe in the name of God come here here is that poor black men those thieving scroundrells took by here this morning with his head half shot off but living. I again asked him to knock me in the head. He says no I wont do that but I will put you in the road where if you have any folks you will be found and they will hear of you if you live or die. I then asked him if he could take care of me. He says no Billy Shores where you passed this morning you know

they accused him of reporting bushwhackers and threatened to shoot him. They took me and laid me in the road
and told me that was the straight road to Winchester. I
asked them which way it was and they said your head is
lying straight toward Winchester. I then crawled off in
the direction indicated until I came to a plank fence. I felt
along the fence until I found a gate. I shook the gate and
called and asked them to please to let me come in and
warm and lie down the woman replied that she would
not as the Bushwhackers would find it out and burn her
house. I lay there at the gate some time and asked her to
allow me to crawl around the back part of the house and
hide as I was afraid the Bushwhackers would come down
the road and find me and kill me. She replied she could
not help that and she would rather I would get away from
the gate. I then started and crawled on. After crawling
some considerable distance a man passed me in a buggy.
I called to him and asked if he would please to take me in
the buggy and take me to Winchester. He replied that he
would not as the Guerrillas would think he was taking
sides with the Yankees and destroy his property and
passed on. I then crawled on as far as I could until I gave
out. I then laid myself down beside a fence after lying
there some time a woman came along who I recognized
by the face to be Mrs McGee and exclaimed William in
the name of God is that you they have treated so. I told
her it was. I then asked her who she was. She replied it is
Mrs McGee don't you know me. I asked her if she would
not have me taken care of. She replied that she would.
She walked off some distance and called Mr Volley
Henderson, he came and she told him to look in the name
of God Almighty how that poor man is abused he replied
Yes, I see its awful that our country is going on at such a
rate. She told him then that I must be taken care of and
sent to Decherd or to Winchester and asked him if he
would not assist, he replied that he had property and that

he feared the Bushwhackers. Then a man came along in a buggy who they called Hosea Green. Mr Henderson asked him to let him have the buggy to take this boy down to Wm Estells or some other physician in Winchester he replied he would not as he had property and they would blame him for taking sides with the Yankees and destroy it. Mrs McGee then asked him in the Name of God Almighty why if he had no human feeling she wished to God she were a man, she would have that buggy. Mr Henderson then called to his brother Mark to step there a minute his brother Mark came when he exclaimed Brother do you see the fix this man is in! He (Mark) replied I do but it is better than expected when I heard they had him. Volley Henderson then said I want you to assist to take this buggy to take this man to Winchester, his brother then said ask him no questions about it, make him light out of there! Green then gave the buggy up and I was placed in it and taken to Winchester by Mr Henderson's orders. They drove me into Winchester and took me out of the buggy and laid me on the side walk in front of the house in which I lived. Dr Sheppard came along and when he saw me volunteered his services, had me removed in to the house and dressed my wounds and attended upon me regularly until I was removed to Decherd by orders of Thomas Wood special Agent, in order to avoid being killed by the Guerrillas as they had sent word they was coming there to kill me. The doctor there took charge of me until I was able to move about, which was some two months afterward. Thos Woods, Wm Jones, and Albert Custer furnished me with money which I was in need of and treated me very kindly also. A. Jordan Post Sutler furnished me with money·

William Huddleston X his mark[41]

Dr. J. C. Shapard was the physician who treated Huddleston. He relates:

I knew nothing of the capture and whipping of Huddleston until after the party capturing him had left town, as I was in bed asleep at the time of those occurrences. I was awakened on that morning by some member of my family who had already risen, and informed me that a party of men, who looked like Confederate soldiers, were hurriedly passing in the street in front of my house with a negro man. I arose and hastily put on my clothes and walked out in front of my house, but before I got out of my room the party was so far off that I could not distinguish who any one of them was and consequently did not know that the negro was William Huddleston.

About the middle of the day I was informed that Huddleston had returned home badly wounded, and I was requested to visit him professionally, which I did immediately. I found him suffering with what I considered an extremely dangerous wound, the ball having entered his head above his right eye, had passed through the intermediate parts, and was lodged in his throat near his jugular vein. Since he could speak only imperfectly at that time he could not give me any satisfactory information about how far he had been taken, who had shot him, or how he got back home.

I think he remained under my care about two weeks, after which, being much improved, and not consider himself safe outside of the Federal lines, he went to Decherd, since which I have seldom seen him.

While he was here under my care, regarding his case as one of extreme danger, I frequently invited the other physicians of the place to visit him with me, which they invariable did with the utmost cheerfulness. Many citizens likewise visited him, during his confinement here, and spoke kindly and pleasantly to him

J.C. Shapard[42]

Huddleston was singled out by the guerrillas because he was employed by the U.S. Army in guiding "scouts," as the expeditions to seize food, forage, and to burn houses were called. Without local cooperation these expeditions would have been considerably less effective, so William Huddleston was seized as an example which would frighten off others who had similar inclinations. The effectiveness of these tactics is evident in the remarks of the whites who showed some human sympathy for Huddleston as he attempted to make his way back to Winchester, but who also feared retribution if they appeared to "side with the Yankees." This incident indicates the narrowness of the area under the control of the Union occupation forces. Decherd Station is located about two miles from the town square in Winchester, but the Union garrison in Decherd had to endure guerrilla activity within sight of their fortifications around the depot. The railroad corridor was narrow and Union control beyond that corridor was uncertain.

The fate of the guerrillas who fell into the hands of Milroy and his forces was uncertain at best. Peter and Joel Cunningham, two brothers who would later become a cause célèbre lived along the spur railway line which ran from Decherd to Fayetteville in the village of Cunningham Station, now known as Flintville. Prior to the war, Peter was clerk of the court of Lincoln County and Joel was a successful farmer and businessman, who operated a store and grist mill in Cunningham Station. Both brothers enlisted in Peter Turney's 1st Tennessee Infantry Regiment which was formed for Confederate service even before the state of Tennessee seceded from the Union. The First Tennessee was sent to Virginia and served with the Army of Northern Virginia for the duration of the war. Sometime in early 1862, the brothers were discharged from Confederate service and returned to Lincoln County. When the Union army invaded the area for the first time following the battle of Shiloh in April 1862, the Cunningham mill was burned and considerable forage and food were seized by the invading forces. When the Union army began its retreat in response to the Confederate advance into Kentucky during the fall of 1862 the Cunninghams organized their neighbors and ambushed stragglers from the Union column.

Although the brothers had been discharged from Confederate military service, they continued to defend the Confederacy on a regional level, in their particular geographic area. When the Tullahoma campaign brought the Union army back to Middle Tennessee the brothers enlisted in the ranks of Lemuel Mead's 4th Alabama Cavalry. Joel rose to the rank of captain while Peter remained a private.

By the late winter of 1864–65 it was obvious to the Cunninghams that the war was over and the South had lost. No doubt Confederate defeat weighed heavily on them, but of greater concern was the lasting damage that was being inflicted by the sheer lawlessness running rampant over their section as former guerrillas and irregular soldiers were joined by deserters from both armies to form outlaw bands. Feeling they could do nothing more for the Confederacy, the brothers decided to do what they could for their home county. To that end, they contacted Lieutenant Colonel W. J. Cliff, the Federal officer commanding the garrison in their county seat.

> Fayetteville Tenn Feb 3d 1865
>
> I have the honor to report that Capt Cunningham of Meads command sent in a proposition to me yesterday to surrender himself and bring in all of his men that he could vouch for and to aid me in putting down the robbing and bushwhacking in this county.
>
> I accepted this proposition and he and his brother surrendered to me last night. I gave the surrender the appearance of a capture and wish it so understood until the objects contemplated can be accomplished.
>
> Capt. Cunningham has given me some valuable information and promises to aid in arranging matters to capture or kill the bands of robbers in the county and I

have reason to think he will do so, for the best citizens here represent him as a man of his word.

The citizens are quiet and orderly and seem anxious to have me remain and protect them from the robbers.

W.J. Cliff Lieut Col Comdg[43]

The Cunninghams gave their word, in the form of a parole, not to oppose the United States in any way. The parole the Cunninghams signed was a common form of allowing prisoners to resume a normal life without going to prison camps. Although the exchange of prisoners had broken down at the national level in 1863, local commanders continued to use paroles throughout the war. The parole the Cunninghams signed said:

I, Peter Cunningham, hereby give my parole of honor, that I will not bear arms against the U.S. Govt, nor help, aid, or assist either directly or indirectly, any person or persons, in making war against the same, that I will not communicate to any person, either directly or indirectly, any information, received while within the Federal lines detrimental to the same; that I will not write nor go into any section of the country in possession of the enemy without written permission of the authorities of the U.S. until regularly exchanged as a prisoner of war; and that I will report in person to W.J. Cliff Lt. Col 5th Tenn Cavy once every week until further orders.

Peter Cunningham[44]

The parole signed by Joel is identical in language and form.

Thirty-five miles away in Tullahoma, General Milroy was not impressed by the report that the Cunninghams had surrendered, and that under the terms of their parole were helping Cliff pacify the county. Milroy had already issued orders stating that the Cunningham brothers were notorious guerrillas who were to be killed on sight. Orders to kill the brothers had been given to Lieutenant Colonel Stauber of the 42nd

Captain Joel Cunningham, CSA

Milroy tried to ignore Cunningham's parole and to have the captain killed.

From a Pencil Sketch in the Author's Collection

Chockley Tavern, Wartrace, Tennessee

This antebellum building was a witness to the numerous guerrilla raids which targeted a crucial section of the N&C Railroad.

Photograph by Author

Missouri as he left on his second house burning and execution patrol. These orders were issued at virtually the same time the Cunninghams surrendered. Although some considered a parole to be legal and moral protection from further action, Milroy did not. Milroy wanted the Cunninghams dead. Accordingly, orders were given to Stauber to send a detachment to Fayetteville to seize the Cunninghams. Suspecting that Cliff might resist such an order, Milroy included in Stauber's instructions permission to relieve Cliff from command if he resisted Milroy's wishes. A member of Cliff's command happened to be in the village of Mulberry when Stauber and his patrol of the 42nd Missouri arrived while on their way to Fayetteville. In a conversation with the Missouri troops, Cliff's man learned of the purpose of Stauber's expedition. Dashing back to Fayetteville he warned Cliff, and when Stauber arrived he found Cliff was ready for him.

Colonel Stauber gave Cliff General Milroy's written order to turn the Cunninghams over to Stauber for delivery to the stockade in Tullahoma. Cliff refused to obey this order and a considerable amount of argument ensued between the two officers. Because he was unable to convince Cliff otherwise, the order relieving him from command in Fayetteville was handed to the commander of the 5th Tennessee. Cliff was directed to report in person to Milroy in Tullahoma on the following day. Cliff stated that his reason for not turning over the prisoners was his fear that Colonel Stauber would kill both the Cunninghams on the way to Tullahoma. Cliff had given his word of honor to protect the two when they signed their paroles and he felt obligated to uphold that commitment. Stauber said he would make sure the Cunninghams were well taken care of, but Cliff put no credence in these words.[45]

The argument that he had pledged his honor to the Cunninghams was precisely the point raised by Cliff, neither did he stop there. Lieutenant Colonel Cliff had been active in Tennessee politics for years prior to the war and had been among the prominent men who spoke out against secession. At almost 70 years of age he was clearly too old for a field command but he insisted on holding one anyway. With this kind of personal determination, and his political connections to both the governor of the state, William Brownlow, and the vice president of the United States, Andrew Johnson, William Cliff was a man to be reckoned with, despite the gap in rank between him and Major General Robert Milroy. Cliff was quick to register his objections with his superior officer through the division adjutant, Captain O. T. Wells. Wells, and the division commander, were located in Pulaski, Tennessee, an area outside Milroy's area of command. By sending the Cunninghams there, Cliff was keeping them safe. Cliff recounted the manner in which he had arranged the surrender of the Cunningham brothers by making it appear they had been captured. He then reiterated that their commanding officer, Lemuel Mead, "had left this part of the country and that they were tired of the war and wished to quit, the Capt also stated he would use his knowledge of the men of his command that had confidence in, and that he would take hold with me, and use to kill out the bushwhackers and robbers in his and adjoining counties." Cliff then recounted that within days Joel Cunningham had helped his forces to take several horses and mules, seize weapons, and capture prisoners while scattering a band of bushwhackers completely. Then the detachment from the 42d Missouri had arrived and ordered him to hand over his prisoners. "I was given to understand that they were to be shot. This as a man of honor I would not allow, until they had been tried for they have carried out their part of the contract with fidelity. I have been relieved from command of the Post at this place and ordered to report to Gen Milroy' s Head Qrs. I understand from the officer handing me the order that if I had allowed the Cunninghams to be taken from me I would not have been relieved. I make this report to you, that you may have a fair understanding of the matter and that you may know how to treat the Cunninghams when they report to you."[46]

Cliff not only disobeyed the order to hand over Peter and Joel, he helped them escape. The two brothers were in the house of Dr. Bonner where Cliff made his personal quarters. This house was on the public square and the Provost Marshal Office was in the courthouse. While he was arguing with Lieutenant Colonel Stauber, Cliff sent word to the Cunninghams to leave town and to report to Union officials in Pulaski, outside Milroy's jurisdiction. Aided, it is said, by young ladies of the town who invited Lieutenant Colonel Stauber and his officers to dinner, the two brothers quietly left Dr. Bonner's house by the back door, crossed Elk River, and disappeared into a tangle of woods which had been struck by a tornado a year or so before and which was much grown up in brush and briars. There they hid out until they could make their way to Pulaski.[47] Cliff then proceeded to gather information to use to prefer charges against Milroy for mistreatment of prisoners and for murder.

Clift also went to work gathering letters of support for his position. Officers from the companies of the 5th Tennessee stationed in Fayetteville generally supported his actions and were willing to say so in writing:

> Camp 5th Tenn Vol Cav
> Fayetteville Tenn Feb 18th 1865
>
> Maj B.G. Polk AAC
> We the undersigned Commissioned officers of the 5th Tenn Cav beg leave to state for the information of the Maj Genl commanding that Joel Cunningham and brother surrendered themselves, horses, arms, &c, to Lt. Col. Clift with the express understanding that their lives and liberty should be protected, giving word promising on their part to prove their faith and allegiance to the U.S. government by taking an active part in scouting the country in connection with this Regt, and to assist in every possible manner to rid the country of Guerrillas. The Cunninghams have since their surrender been the means of several others

coming in with their arms &c. Lt. Col. Clift pledged his word and honor for their safety and on his making this sacred promise several prominent citizens pledged their lives and property for the good faith of the said Cunninghams, to the consideration of several officers of the 5th Tenn Cav all of whom heartily endorsed the Cols policy in accepting his surrender. Today Col Clift received an order from Maj Gen Milroy to deliver the Cunninghams into the hands of Lt. Col. T.J. Stauber, 42nd Missouri Vols.

Accompanying the first order was a second to the effect that in the event of Col Clift refusing to obey the first, he was relieved of the command of this post and ordered to report in person at Head Qrs N&C RR. Defs., Tullahoma, Tenn. Col Clift having heard that in all probability it was the intention to execute the Cunninghams and having pledged his sacred word and honor to protect them from harm upon the conditions before mentioned refused to deliver them up.

S. Waters, Maj 5 Tenn Cav   Robt E. Gavin Capt Co G
Peter Cason Capt Co L   W.O. Richman Capt Co H
R.C. Couch Capt Co F   Edward H. Cossen 1 Lt Co B
J.W. Bryson 2 Lt Co B   W.G. Davis 1 Lt Co A
W.R. Hough 1 Lt Co A & Act Adjt
Chas H. Stewart 1 Lt & RQM   W.T. Harrison 2 Lt Co C
L.W. Mallard 1 Lt Co C[48]

In addition to the officers of the 5th Tennessee, prominent local civilians wrote to Brigadier General R. W. Johnson in command at Pulaski, asking that the Cunninghams be protected. J. Y. Gordon, clerk of the county court, admitted that Lincoln county had gained a bad name for being overrun with outlaws and guerrillas but that the people were tired of the situation and desired to improve things. He pointed out that the 5th Tennessee Cavalry, commanded by Colonel Cliff, had been in Fayetteville for some time and that Cliff had come up with a very successful plan to catch the worst of the outlaws who had been present in the area for at least three years. This plan revolved around the involvement of the Cunningham brothers. Since they had been allowed to give their parole and to begin cooperating with the Union forces, eight of the worst outlaws had been killed and some 30 others had been captured. A great many others who were not involved in crimes but only in military activities had been encouraged to give themselves up. Mr. Young protested strongly against Milroy's actions in insisting that the Cunninghams be sent to Tullahoma and relieving Cliff of command. Cliff, he said, had "done more to change public opinion in favor of the U.S. government than all the efforts of the war in our county."[49]

Not surprisingly, Milroy did not react mildly to this challenge to his orders and his will concerning the Cunninghams. Lieutenant Colonel Cliff had charges and specifications placed against him for disobedience of orders and assisting prisoners to escape. In preparation for his trial before a court-martial the lieutenant colonel continued to amass evidence against Milroy which would, he felt, justify his actions in helping the Cunninghams leave Fayetteville, not as escaped prisoners, but as exiles who had merely gone to a Union officer who was trustworthy and had there placed themselves back in custody. In writing to General W. D. Whipple, chief of staff of General George Thomas, Cliff reviewed the circumstances under which the Cunninghams gave their parole, the attempt to remove them from his custody, and then offered reasons why he thought Milroy was not to be trusted with prisoners.

> . . . I wish to state a few facts in order that you may judge whether I had a right to fear the Cunninghams would be unjustly dealt with. Therefore what I have to state occurred after I was relieved from command; it is therefore what I heard after I was relieved. On the 27th day of Feby six prisoners were shot at Tullahoma and on the 3rd day of March more yet I rode out in company with Lt Davis 5th TVC and found them lying in the woods

unburied without anything around them to prevent the
hogs from tearing their corpses to pieces. Capt — —, 59th
Ohio Inf supplied him with the names of the men and
showed him the general report. Their names were as follows: William Wilcher, Calvin Cox, Samuel Smith, John
Pursley, G.W. Sanders, B.F. Darring. On the Guard Book
they were reported as having been shot while attempting
to escape. I have positive proof and will produce it if necessary. A prisoner by the name of Nelson who was captured by command and confined in the guard house at
Fayetteville was released to Capt Sparks of the Homeguard
on orders from Lt. Col. Stauber to convey him to some
secret place and shoot him. Captain Sparks informed me
that he complied with the order. John Morton formerly of
the 16th Ala Inf (Rebels) bushwhacker operating in Lincoln County Tenn told me that Jones was a notorious thief
and bushwhacker and then surrendered himself arms,
horse, and horse equipment to me at Headquarters. When
he came in he gave information of a party of Guerrillas
and I sent a scout immediately and found the facts as
stated. I paroled him to take the oath and retained him as
a guide. Lt. Col. Stauber, when I was relieved, arrested
him and carried him to Tullahoma where he was confined
in the stockade. I went to Tullahoma and made applica-
tion to the Pro Mar on Gen Milroy' Staff to have him retained as a witness before my court martial but on the
2nd or 3rd day of March he disappeared from the Stockade. I do not think he escaped but I have reason to believe
he met the fate of the others. Other facts might be stated
to show the illegal and barbarous course pursued toward
prisoners but pursuing the above will suffice. If I had been
called on to deliver the Cunninghams into the hands of a
man who did not deal unjustly and illegally with prisoners I would have immediately complied with the order. I
honestly thought that if I handed them over to death their
blood would be upon my hands.[50]

The accusations of Colonel Cliff were supported by a letter from James Chadd, a discharged soldier who had continued to work at Tullahoma as an army employee. In his letter Chadd said:

> On or about the 6th day of Feby 1865 there were two men shot at Tullahoma, and on the 20th of January Capt Lewis and Capt Peter Thompson 42d Mo Infy shot three men, two of the men who were shot were named Sanders and the other a gray headed man whose name I have forgotten. The last three men I know to have been shot by Gen Milroys orders. I saw the order myself it was signed by Gen Milroy and ordered Capt Lewis to burn certain houses and kill certain men. I was at that time Wagon Master and had twelve wagons on a Scout with Capt Lewis. The wagons were loaded with the household furniture of the men who were shot consisting of beds, bedsteads, clocks, chairs, pots, lard, black smiths tools, whisky, molasses, and personal clothing which was hauled to Tullahoma. I do not know what disposition was made of the articles. The men who were shot were citizens and lived in Coffee county and none of them were armed.
>
> On or about the 23d of Feby 1865 I saw ten men shot at Tullahoma. The men who shot them told me it was by Gen Milroys orders. They had been confined in the Stockade and were taken out and shot.
>
> On the 2d or 3d of March I came up to a party of soldiers about fifteen minutes after they had shot a man. They told me they had him there chopping wood and that Gen Milroy had ordered him shot. The guard said he was shot while chopping. From the description you gave me of John Morton a rebel soldier, I believe he was the man who was shot. My residence is Calhoun, Kentucky, I was a private in the 2d Kentucky Artillery mustered out at the expiration of my term of enlistment and then employed as Post Wagon Master at Tullahoma, Tenn.[51]

This document was sworn and subscribed before E. R. Campbell, commissioner of the U.S. Circuit Court for the Middle District of Tennessee.

The evidence Cliff amassed in his defense made Milroy look quite bad since his actions in killing prisoners without trial and without the sentences being approved at a higher headquarters were in direct violation of General Orders No. 100 which laid out the procedure to be followed in dealing with guerrillas and bushwhackers. General Thomas apparently did not want the matter to be dealt with publicly because he knew of Milroy's political connection. In due course the charges against Lieutenant Colonel Cliff were shelved and lost in a deliberate bureaucratic tangle and the colonel never got to make public his charges against Milroy. This does not mean Milroy ceased his policy of quick revenge against those he found in arms against him. He simply left more of the action to others and did not put as much in the army's official record. His diary and his letters home, however, show that "blood and fire" continued to be his policy.

In the northeastern corner of Milroy's area of responsibility, around the town of McMinnville, guerrillas carried on a lively activity, sometimes successful for them, sometimes losing to the U.S. forces. As late as February 1865, skirmishes were taking place. Captain H. N. Woley of the 42nd Missouri reported he had come across about one hundred guerrillas commanded by a man named Purdham.

> We followed them all day, or until about 3 p.m., when we came in on their camp in the mountains. They had picked their position and had made a good selection, and were it not for their condition they might have held their position for a while. They were posted along a gulch running south to the brow of a hill. They were also in line along the hill. As Captain Lewis came up in the advance they poured a heavy fire into our advance as we ascended the hill where they were posted. Most of our officers being in

the front, Capt. M.M. Floyd, of the Fifth Tennessee Cavalry, was severely wounded, also two soldiers belonging to the same regiment. The boys of the forty-second were uninjured, except by slight scratches and bullet holes in their clothes. The rebels left so rapidly that it was impossible for us, on worn-out horses, to overtake them. On examination we found two dead horses, and from indications two men were killed or severely wounded and taken off the field by their comrades. Capt Lewis says he can hold the country and scatter the rebels all through. he thinks a few more of the Forty-second would be acceptable, as the home guards will not all do to tie to. We go to McMinnville from here.[52]

The tide was turning against the guerrillas, and more of them began to be captured, and to face the uncertain mercies of a court-martial. Among the guerrillas operating around McMinnville were Slocum Brown, Isaac Brown, Green Brown, Frank Brown, John Brown, and Charles Eddings. These men all had family ties with each other, raising the prospect that their guerrilla activities may have been connected to personal grudges against their victims. These men were caught and brought before a court-martial where they were charged with the murder of Raphael Tidwell whom they had poisoned, and with the attempted murder of Negroes living on a farm called the Durley Place. They had also stolen tobacco, leather, meat, and clothes from Ann Tidwell, widow of Raphael, and had robbed the Negroes of $25 and the clothes they had been issued as employees of the United States government.[53]

Charles Eddings had operated on his own as an outlaw before joining the Browns. He was charged by the court-martial with "the intention to rob, plunder, and murder peaceable and loyal citizens of the United States." Eddings had aided the Browns in committing murder, it was charged, and had also acted as a guerrilla against U.S. soldiers. Frequently he was said to have acted as a guide, leading guerrillas to the home of

Union men so they could be robbed. Specifically, Eddings had robbed Orenton Hammonds of $25 and "a quantity of wearing apparel" as well as participating in the robbery of Ann Tidwell.[54]

One of the witnesses against the gang, G. W. Smith, said:

> I live in sight of Mr. G.W. Durley residence and herd the shooting of guns and hollowing on the evening of the twenty third of January and in about two hours after I saw Herman one of the black boys who had been badly hurt on his head and his body was badly bruised by blows from a gun. I am acquainted with the general character of Green Brown, Isaac Brown, and Charles Eddings and it is very bad why they have been a terror to the citizens of Warren Co for 20 years previous to this time.[55]

Sometimes the would-be robbers more than met their match. P. W. Myers of Warren County said that on the last day of January 1865, he saw L. B. Rodgers and James Tallman pass his house on the road to McMinnville. They seemed to be in a great hurry and requested Myers not to tell anyone he had seen them go by. The next day a Negro girl, a slave to his neighbor, C. Parks, came to Myers and requested him to come to Parks' house since it was under attack by robbers. While Myers was getting together his weapons and ammunition, Rodgers, Green Brown, Isaac Brown, and an unknown man came up from the direction of Parks' house in a great hurry. They admitted they had attacked Parks and that he and his neighbors had gotten the best of them. They wanted Myers to go to Parks and get their horses and said that if their horses were returned they would leave Parks alone, if not they would return to the attack. However, they added, if the horses were not returned, would Parks at least send their blankets. On delivering this message Myers was told to take the horses back to the men since Parks did not want them, but to tell the robbers to leave Parks alone in the future.[56] The matter of losing all the horses belonging to the gang and leaving behind their bedrolls to boot makes the guerrillas look almost comical, except they carried guns and would have used them, had the chance arisen. These were, after all, some of the same men who had killed Raphael Tidwell and who had robbed his widow as well as attacking a party of Negroes.

One guerrilla who was somewhat more dangerous than the Greens was Absalom Ware. In the testimony given against him it was said that he was in a raid made by guerrillas on McMinnville in October 1864. This raid was led by a Captain Carter and resulted in stores and private houses being robbed as well as other depredations. Ware came back with another guerrilla raid on Christmas Day 1864, this time under the command of a Captain Ricketts. This time several houses were burned and a Union soldier named David Blackwell was captured, led out of town, and shot. Thomas Chastain and a Mr. Lively lived near Blackwell and saw the capture and saw Ware accompany the party which led Blackwell away. Shortly after the Christmas raid, on January 3, 1865, Ware was seen by Samuel Pennebaker taking shots across the river at Union pickets guarding the town. Later, Ware was heard boasting that he had killed "one damned Yankee." That same day Ware robbed James Madden of his pocket book and money, as well as taking his roan horse. Then he entered the house of S. M. Scott, broke open a chest, and took silver knives, forks, and spoons, along with other housewares. On another occasion, two mules had been taken from the barn of Harding Patterson. Patterson tracked the mules and found them in the possession of Ware.[57]

Another hard-case lot was William Wilcher who seems to have led a life of crime before the war and who then used the social unrest of the war years as a good opportunity to further his criminal career. Following his arrest, several witnesses appeared against Wilcher, including Mrs. Martha Nunley. Mrs. Nunley said, "I have known William Wilcher for the last ten years — He has born the character of a very bad man ever since I have known him. He is a thief and a robber of the worst kind." On the 20th of August, 1864, Wilcher had stolen a cow from her, killed and butchered the cow, and then brought the meat to her house, offering to sell it to her. While the Union forces were in McMinnville, Wilcher hid out in the woods, but when the Bushwhackers came into the area he came out and joined them. Then, when the Bushwhackers left, Wilcher went back to hiding in the woods. She concluded, "without any exception I think William Wilcher was the worst Bushwhacker and thief that ever came to this locality."[58]

Rustling cows and selling beef appears to have been a favorite activity of Wilcher's. Mrs T. C. Harrison, a citizen of McMinnville, said, "I have known Wm Wilcher by character for many years — he has born a very disreputable character ever since I first heard of him." In August 1864, Wilcher had come to town, took one of her beef cows, killed it and refused to pay her for it. "I have always heard of him as being a very bad character — and a worthless man." Wilcher had accompanied one of the guerrilla raids into McMinnville. On that occasion he had gotten the keys to the railroad depot from Mrs. Harrison's grandson. "In this Depot there was a wagon which had been sent from the north. William Wilcher took this wagon from the Depot and sold it." Samuel Henderson noted of Wilcher that "When he was quite a boy he robbed the United States Mail and was sent to the Penitentiary and after 3 years stayed there he was reprieved by Pres Jackson."[59]

Obviously, the bushwhacking life attracted some who had made a life of crime, petty and otherwise. Wilcher was a rather old man if he was pardoned by President Andrew Jackson. "Old Hickory" left office in 1836 and Wilcher, by that time, had already attacked and been convicted of robbing the U.S. mails.

As attacks continued against the guerrillas, and their supporters, real and imagined, arrests were made and innocent people were caught in Milroy's net. These, under military law, had to prove their innocence. Women were not exempt from arrest under these circumstances. The following case is typical of many.

Jany 30, 1865

To the Provost Marshal General Tullahoma

Sir, I sent tonight two prisoners who were captured this morning a little before day break at the house of one Kelly, about 7 miles beyond Winchester. Their names are John Ragan and Samuel Nance. They were according to all the information I can get among the murderers of the colored man Preston Pierce who was killed on the 22nd. Two others named Temple and Rogers were engaged with them. They admitted to me to day that they had been present with Temple and Rogers and that the latter killed the man, but that they were not present at that time. The real truth is they were all together according to the best information I can get. These men are also reported to be notorious bushwhackers and murderers before this last murder.

I send Kelly and his wife along, for the reason they were represented to me as voluntarily harboring and concealing these men. Some of their neighbors are ready to vouch for their loyalty, and claim that the bushwhackers forced themselves upon them. I leave that for your determination. The horses, arms, & accouterments of the bushwhackers were captured & brought in and will be turned over to the proper officers.

Byrin Paine Lt Col 43 PRO VI
Comdt Post[60]

Mrs. Kelly defended herself with this account:

I reside about six miles below Winchester Franklin County Tenn. I am married. My husbands name is Luke Kelly. On or about sundown of the 20 of Jany 1865 two men named John Reagan and Sam Nance rode up to the house dismounted and entered the house by the back door said

they wanted to see Kelly to induce him to go see Mr
Gillespie to induce him to intercede for them to see if they
could get out of bushwhacking. I told them Kelly my husband would not be at home that night. They said they
were going to stay at my house. I answered they could
not that my husband was not at home. They said they
would stay. After Kelly came home they requested him to
intercede for them in order that they might return to their
home. They then laid down by the fire and remained in
that position until the Federal soldiers arrived a little before day. They surrounded the house and told me to make
a light. They then come in the house and asked if any Bushwhackers were in the house. I told them there is and they
inquired where. I said in the next room. The Lt asked me
if i had taken the Oath I stated I had not. The men who
were in the house made some show of resistance but were
overpowered by the soldiers. After doing this the Federal
soldiers asked if I could fix breakfast for them. I said I
thought I could if they would help me. They assisted me
in fixing the fire and such and that is all the conversation
I recall at present as passing between myself and the soldiers mentioned. As soon as they took breakfast they left
with their prisoners. They brought my husband and myself along with them. They asked me after I stated that
Kelly was not at home for the Bushwhackers being there.
That is all I remember of the conversation.

      Matilda Jane Kelly[61]

The Kellys were released and it was Reagan and Nance whom
Milroy had standing on the scaffold with ropes around their
necks when an order arrived from Nashville informing him
he had to give men a trial before executing them. Of course,
the Kellys were found in suspicious circumstances, but suspicion was easily aroused in the minds of provost marshals. On
occasion the fact that one knew a guerrilla and wished to show
common decency toward their dead bodies was enough to
cause an investigation.

On February 20, 1865, a guerrilla raid was made on the village of Wartrace. This village was a rail junction where a spur line to Shelbyville left the main line of the N&C. One of the guerrillas named Van Horton, also known as Trammel, was killed in the raid.[62] On his body was found a Colt army revolver, a pair of saddlebags containing clean shirts and socks, a copy of Shakespeare inscribed "To Mr. Trammel from his friend, Dollie Battle, Rebel Hill, Jany 19, 1865," and an ambrotype of Mrs. Dollie Battle.[63] Soon after receiving this inventory of possessions General Milroy informed Department Headquarters in Nashville that he had under arrest two "noted rebel women," Mrs. Dollie Battle and her daughter, Miss Sallie Battle. The two lived 10 miles from Nashville but had come all the way to Wartrace on horseback to find the body of Van Horton, place it in a coffin, and bury it. Milroy noted that the "daugerrotypes of these two she rebels" had been found on the dead man's body along with letters showing that they were close friends. The women boasted of their Confederate sympathies and said they had never taken the Oath of Allegiance. It was known that the husband and father was an officer in Confederate service and that the son of the family, Bob, was a guerrilla. "Their mother, as I was well informed last summer, boasts that they have done more good for the Confederate cause than a regiment of soldiers. I respectfully ask permission to send these two south of our lines."[64]

General George Thomas replied, asking for more information. The act of desiring to bury a friend was not an act of disloyalty, Thomas said, but he was concerned to know if the Battles had really boasted of being rebels who had never taken the Oath despite living behind Union lines. He continued, "The evidence which you report, however, creates a suspicion that they may have been taking advantage of their position as women and become the colleagues and associates of guerrillas—the most diabolical of all political criminals. If such be clearly the fact they must be sent beyond our lines."[65]

Chief of Army Police Truesdale himself undertook the investigation for Milroy. His report tells an interesting story:

> In obedience to the above order I proceeded on Friday March 31st with Mrs Kate Gannoway of Tullahoma to the above mentioned place. After arriving there I was introduced by Mrs Gannoway to a Mrs Thomas Tarpley being introduced by Mrs Kate Gannoway as an active rebel who also has a husband in the Rebel Army as a good Rebel myself I was at once made a confidant as to the secret operations of Rebel sympathizers in that locality. Upon my alluding to Captain Van Houtens being killed by the Yankees at Wartrace Mrs Tarpley at once dropped into a chair & remarked that it was one of the unfortunate moves of the Confederates at the present time and Doctor Simms was really the instigator of the raid into Wartrace, an explanation to my surprise. Mrs Tarpley said that Genl Forrest had some two months ago sent word to Simms & other past scouts of his between Nashville & Chattanooga to aid in capturing telegraphic instruments for the use of his department. She (Mrs Tarpley) said that Doc Simms thought the proper time had come and had arranged with one of the Tel operators at Wartrace to have everything in readiness on a give day so as to enable the raiders to accomplish their object without suspicion or danger to any of the parties engaged. Unfortunately however Van Houten the Rebel officer in command of the squad drank a little to much rot gut and in consequence disregarded the instructions given him by Doc Simms which resulted in the death of Van Houten and complete failure of the scheme.
>
> Mrs Tarpley also stated that the same night that Van Houten was killed three of his (Van Houtens) men came to her house to ascertain the road to Mr. Ransoms, a noted secessionist as perhaps (according to their own expression) Head Quarters for all good Rebs.

On Monday April 2d I made business to the Telegraph for the purpose of learning which operator at that post was cognizant of and connected with the above mentioned raid. I met Mr Ware in the office and introduced myself and business (pretended) sending a dispatch to some one in Tullahoma and while waiting for an answer the news of the fall of Richmond came over the wires he told me of the news whereupon I seemed gloomy and sad over the misfortune which had just befallen the Confederacy. He seemed to sympathize with me and denounced in the most abusive language Maj Genl Milroy, Major Billings Provost Marshal & all Officers Commanding in the Sub Dist. He alluded to the arrest of one Mr Elkins in particular & citizens generally threatening what he would do in case he was a citizen and said if Elkins was punished for killing Negroes he would be avenged. I spoke of obtaining a pass to Tullahoma for Mrs Tarpley & Mrs Gannoway when he said he could have them brought on a freight train without any pass and said he was doing a good underground business shipping from eighteen to nineteen persons every day to Nashville & other points on the line of the N&C RR. Just at this moment some one came in and we dropped the subject of passes.

After this I introduced the subject of the raid and asked him is he was one of the number captured to which he replied he was and gave a full account of the whole affair, laughed at the good joke on the parties captured and made a good deal of fun about the expression of Mr Thomas face as he woke up in the night of the raid and found a rebel standing over him with a revolver drawn at his head demanding his watch & money. While we were conversing Mrs Kate Gannoway and Mrs Tarpley went to the Post Office. Learning the above after they had gone I spoke in a confidential manner to him (the operator) asking if he could how it was the Captain (meaning Van

Houten) happened to be so foolish as to make such a bold attempt at robbery in Wartrace at that time and he told me that the plan adopted was well arranged and would have been a perfect success had they stopped when they had accomplished what they intended to do. Said he had pleasure of removing the instruments from the table and handing them over to Van Houten and also said that even Thomas thought he seemed satisfied in being so fortunate as to get off with his live was willing to regard the thing as a joke rather severe on them. But when they went elsewhere they made the thing so public that he found it necessary to give the alarm to save himself. Said if he had not given the alarm he would have been suspect himself but if they had gone back in proper time with the instruments alone to Doctor Simms the scheme would have been a perfect success. The Ladies about this time returned and the subject was dropped. After the Ladies again came in I asked him in case I was unable to get a pass from Gen Milroy for Mrs Gannoway and Mrs Tarpley if he would be so kind as to pass them over the road to Tullahoma. He replied that he would secure the passage at either eight o'clock in the morning or at four in the evening. He proposed to Mr Thomas to send them in the Express car as it would be more comfortable than riding in the freight cars or flats, explaining that Mrs Gannoway was a relative of the Express Agent in Tullahoma and Mr Thomas declined saying it was unsafe and he thought it was not proper to do so.

The next day we went to his office between three and four o'clock P.M. for the purpose of securing passage through his agency on a freight train. This took place April 4th. A few minutes before the train from Nashville came along which he said he would send us on Mrs Elkins and daughter arrived on a freight train from Tullahoma. He (operator) told us that he had sent Mrs Elkins and daughter up to Tullahoma in the morning & had them back. We were put on the second train from Nashville by him and came to Tullahoma. No passes were called for by the conductor, before leaving however for Tullahoma the operator spoke of having set traps by which he was going to catch the miserable wharf rats in the shape of Dutch soldiers belonging to the 188th O.V.I. stationed at Wartrace and stated a mode by which he had caught three.[66]

Sometimes those accused of consorting with guerrillas had to turn out large numbers of neighbors to prove their loyalty to the U.S. government. As the provost's net spread wider and wider, attempting to apprehend the disloyal and to stamp out Confederate sympathy, more and more arrests were made of innocent people. In Lincoln County 41 neighbors of Champ Smith signed a document stating that he was "a good and peaceful citizen and since he has taken the Oath of Amnesty to the Government of the United States he has in our opinion conducted himself as a good and loyal citizen and we believe he has respected his said oath in particular and if since the taking of his oath he has been guilty of treason it has been in such things as have not appeared to the public. We do not believe he has been guilty of such acts."[67]

Perhaps the most outrageous case of the wrong person being arrested and her goods seized was the affair which involved Mrs. Virginia Moore and Mrs. Gail Hibbs. In January Milroy ordered the arrest of Mrs. Sarah Moore, a widow, living near Lynchburg.[68] There was a large family of Moores in that area and many of them were strongly pro-Confederate. From Sarah Moore attention shifted to the Mulberry area where Mrs. Virginia Moore lived. Captain John G. Sparks of the Home Guard received orders from Milroy to go on a scout to destroy still houses in the Mulberry area and to be on the lookout for goods taken from the firm of Rudd & Sullivan by guerrillas. The Mulberry area had been a hotbed of guerrillas since 1863, and General Slocum had sent an expedition to the village to collect an indemnity for the death of some of his men. On this expedition Sparks encountered a party led by Lieutenant G. W. Glynn of the 102nd New York Infantry.[69] Sparks said of the subsequent events:

> I started and proceeded to the house of Mrs Hibbs. I was not aware of the precise location of the house. I passed it some 3/10 of a mile when I came up with Lt Glynn who stated I had passed the house. I then proceeded back to the house. Glynn was in the advance and him and his men were in the house when I arrived. I found Glynn and his men rummaging the house. After dismounting I informed my men that they should take anything which would be of use to the Government but not to take any of the women or children clothing and I would report our action to Col Stauber at Fayetteville. We then went into the house and made inquiries as to whether there was any Government stores arms &c. Mrs Hibbs stated there was nothing of the kind there. I then remarked I would have to search the house as that was my orders, and asked her for the keys of the drawers &c. I then proceeded to search the house. I found two boxes marked "Sutlers Goods" and containing muslins, domestics and various articles of merchandise. I came to the conclusion they were contraband of war and proceeded to unpack them. I told the men to pack them up and we would take them to Fayetteville. Geo Farris one of Glynn's men informed that Lt Glynn had two such boxes in his possession and of the 5th Tenn Cav U.S. took a considerable quantity of goods from the house. Lt Glynn has no connection with me, had not been on a Scout under my command. All the goods taken by my order was the contents of the two boxes with the exception of some sugar and coffee and a piece of material which one of my men wanted for a saddle blanket. I pried off the ceiling board for the purpose of ascertaining whether or not property of any kind was concealed

in the cavity between the weather boarding and the ceiling. I told the men to take the goods in the boxes for the purpose of having them taken out and one of my men took a childs hood. After taking the goods we started on our return reported to Col. Stauber our actions and he remarked it was all right to hold on to the goods. Lt Glynn and his men were at the house when I left with my command.

John Sparks X his mark[70]

A neighbor of Gail Hibbs happened to be at her house when Sparks and Glynn arrived and told a somewhat different story. Mrs. Virginia Moore was related to the former attorney general of Tennessee, William Moore, and was living in his house at the time of the incident. Mrs. Moore said:

Major Billings, I presume you have heard of the robbing of Mrs Hibbs house by Federal soldiers under com'd of Capt Sparks & Lt Glynn. I had a few goods there myself which they took. I wish to explain to you how they happened to be there and would be glad to have them returned or paid for, as I find it almost impossible to raise means to supply the necessities of my family. Last August Mrs Hibbs & myself wished to buy some family supplies, salt, dry goods & Mrs Hibbs could not leave her children & I had no wagon suitable, so she furnished wagon, oxen & driver. I rode horseback and purchased the articles for both families. When the wagon returned it stopped at Mrs Hibbs. I told her I would not trouble her to send my box home but let it remain at her house and I would take the articles home in my carpet bag as I needed them. I had brought home most of the articles but those left were the largest bundles & most valuable and I would have brought them all home the evening before they were taken if I could have left home as one of my neighbors had promised to assist me with any sewing as I wished to move farther north if I can get off. Last January 16th Lt

Glynn, Sgt McGowen & several other soldiers rode up to my door. They mostly sat their horses but some walked up to the door and talked 5 or 10 minutes & rode off. Next morning Lt Glynn called alone, came in & sat down a few minutes. A while after he left I heard all the soldiers had gone to Fayetteville. I then rode up to Mrs Hibbs to see her sick children and was greatly surprised on reaching there to see her house & porch full of soldiers with boxes and trunks pulled out in the porch emptying them of their contents. I could not get in at the front door so rode to the back door & called Mrs Hibbs. She came to the door & Lt Glynn came to the door also. He walked out in the yard a few steps & said he would like to speak to me. I rode to where he stood, he then asked me where Mr. H was. I replied on his farm in Alabama, he then said he was a bushwhacker. I told him no, he never had been & that every reliable citizen would clear him of that charge he then said Mrs H fed & harbored bushwhackers & they had brought these goods there. I told him I had no idea one had ever been in her house, it was more than she could do to feed her children well as for the goods I knew they were bought and paid for & had permits to bring them out of Shelbyville the revenue officer at Shelbyville, Capt Ramsy, could show it on his books. Mrs H came up about that time & I asked her where my goods were. She said those men had them. I then described my goods to Lt Glynn & told him how they happened to be there & that I had the bill & permit at home for them. He then remarked he did not think they would take mine and it was very hard to treat Mrs H so but it was Genl Milroys orders to take every thing she had but the wearing clothes for herself & children. Mrs H told him she did not believe Genl Milroy had given any such orders and she intended to write and ask him. I then told him I would go home & send up the bill & permit for my goods as I rode round

the house I saw Capt Sparks cutting the weather boarding off of the house with an ax. Mrs H had told Lt G that
her little son had an old shot gun that Father (Gen Wm
Moore) had borrowed it to kill some birds. Lt G requested
me to hurry home & send him the gun as soon as I reached
home I started a boy with the gun & as soon as I could
find my permit for my goods I gave it to Father to take to
Mrs H & show to Capt S & Lt G but they had left with my
goods before he reached there. Saturday 18th I went to
Fayetteville. Saw Col Stauber & explained my goods being at Mrs H's also had a bill with me but he did not look
at it after I returned home I wrote him but did not know
where to send my letter. Now I understand he is at
Tullahoma so I will include it with this below I will give
you a list of the goods purchased in my name.

Mrs. Moore then listed 52 yards of cloth of various types and
in pieces of various lengths valued at a total of $46.15[71] as be-
ing the property belonging to her which had been taken from
the Hibbs home.

The "permit" spoken of by Virginia Moore was written
permission for civilians to purchase goods for their personal
or family use. It was illegal to shop without such a permit, and
goods for which persons had no permit could be confiscated.
The purpose of the permit system was to prevent civilians from
amassing goods which could then be turned over to guerrillas. Of course, this system also allowed the provost marshal to
deny the right to buy food and clothing to those believed to be
"disloyal."

Mrs. Hibbs also offered testimony about what happened
and what she lost in the search of her house. On February 21,
1865, in a letter to Major A. W. Billings, provost marshal at
Tullahoma, she said:

> I wish to inform you of the conduct of some soldiers
> under command of Capt Sparks & Lt Glynn who visited

my home on last Friday. They came riding down the road very rapidly but I had no idea they were coming in until they rode in —advanced, dismounting at the gate & came rushing in like madmen—two in my room & two in the adjoining. One, Lieut Glynn, in a easy bright manner wanted to know who lived here. I told him Mrs Hibbs, he then inquired for Mr Hibbs. I told him he was in Ala on his farm. In fairly rough language he said it was well known he was a bushwhacker. By this time the room was full—the Lieut ordering them to go to work. He then said he had orders from Genl Milroy for the delivery of all the arms in the house, which I gave up—two old holster pistols used in the Mexican war & a small shot gun. The Capt & his men in the meantime were taking everything they could find in the adjoining rooms while another party up stairs, was ripping & looting everything in their way. I had bought a supply of clothing for myself & children six in number, but owing to sickness in my family for six months had been unable to make it up. When questioned about the cloth I was unable to produce the permits for it, having carelessly mislaid them. I told them emphatically that a bushwhacker had never entered my house, so help me God, whereas they were in it then. This they knew to be a fact but they would send to their Captain & have his opinion. He came staggering in and after looking at one or two dress patterns said "help yourselves, boys" No sooner said than done and in a few minutes every yard of goods, some that I had made at home, was gone, so that I have not a decent suit of clothing for my children. They did not leave a blanket in the house, and barely enough covering for two beds—took all my coffee & sugar except a few pounds. I enclose a list of the articles as far as I can. Capt Sparks, I think, then got an ax & commenced cutting away the ceiling & weather boarding standing at the head of my bed—searching for money I suppose. I have since understood that the greatest charge they had against me was that I had six kegs of white lead which my husband had bought in 1861 for the purpose of painting a house he had purchased near Shelbyville but had been prevented in consequence of the war—for this I refer you to W.W. Gate of Bedford Co. I can also refer you to other reliable citizens in regard to Mr Hibbs being a bushwhacker—he has never been engaged in this war, but has been living quietly on his farm in Ala in the hope of paying his debts. After all the damage was done Lt Glynn apologized, regretting that he was under the necessity of fulfilling such orders from Genl Milroy but that he was only obeying orders of a person higher than himself. I told them I should write & inform Genl Milroy that his orders if such they were, had been carried out to perfection. Tho I cannot believe that any officer of position and standing in the Federal army ever issued any such orders. I took the Oath of Allegiance, readily & freely, & have never violated it, at the same time receiving protection for my person & property. Hoping I have not intruded upon your tome & that you will inquire into this affair and have my property restored or compensated in some way. I am respectfully

J. Gail Hibbs

PS On their returning in the evening, they halted in front of my house, some of them presenting guns & some rode up to the door, with pistols drawn—wanting to know if there was not a man in that house. I pointed to my little son, telling that this was the only man here, upon which they rode off.

JGH

They broke open all the locks after I had given up the keys & when they found a trunk they could not break the lock of they smashed it open. They also took the likeness of my deceased brother & sister, also one of my sister, Mrs J.B. Smith & some old sabers they found, used in the Mexican War. Not knowing the soldiers were here, Mrs Moore came up to see my sick child. Lieut Glynn came to the door & then rode up & then inquired what she was engaged at, told him she had some goods & horses, explaining why they happened to be here, & that she would present her permits. By then they had left with the goods, before she arrived. Mrs Moore & my children are the only witnesses to the same.

JGH

There follows a list of the goods taken from the house. The list is somewhat lengthy but it has a strong emotional impact when read, as well as being of historical value. From the list one learns what a typical Civil War era housewife had on hand to clothe her family. One can also see how thoroughly looters proceeded, even to stealing sewing needles. It has little effect to read a brief sentence saying that a house was looted; a different experience is produced when one sees the details of the loss. Mrs. Hibbs listed as lost:

1 fine gray shawl—9 blankets—5 quilts
4 yds checked brown silk   3 yds gray poplin
3 yds brown calico with small red figure   1 yd red flannel
1 yd black silk   3 yds white cotton
16 yds Jess calico, red & black spots
16 yds bead calico, white & black spots
12 yds denim, white & black spots
10 yds dark calico, red flowers   11 yds denim, red palms
10 yds light English calico, black trees and brown flowers
2 1/2 yds dotted Swiss muslin   4 yds light spotted muslin
4 yds light muslin, brown squares 10 or 12 yds gray & plaid cottonade
4–5 yds blue & brown corse homespun 7 yds white linsey
5 yds white linsey   3 yds gray casmier   12 yds brown domestic
3 linen table cloths   8 linen towels   8 linen handkerchiefs

1/2 lb black flax   2 doz spools — candlesticks — needles —
tape — buttons — ribbons — pins
2 worsted hoods   Boys pants & shirts   Sheets & pillow cases
1 coral necklace   Brushes & combs   Gold watch — ring —
bracelets — breast pin
30 lb coffee   20 lbs sugar   20 yds black calico
26 yds black domestic   2 1/2 yds table linen
4 yds linen toweling   1 dozen table napkins
J Gail Hibbs [72]

In this final flurry of revenge at the end of the war even idle gossip and loose talk was enough to get a person reported to the provost for investigation. Miss Mollie Smith was traveling by wagon, in company with several other people, from Murfreesboro to McMinnville on April 20, 1865. One of her fellow travelers, Louis Meadows, was offended by Miss Smith's "politically incorrect" speech. He said, "we had come a few miles from Woodbury in this direction Miss Mollie Smith commenced talking very disrespectfully about the Yankees." The other passengers tried to dissuade her from her tirade, telling her that she might marry such a person, but " She (Miss Smith) replied that if a Yankee was to offer such a thing she would cut his throat. She said that before she would marry a Yankee she would die an old maid and turn to a whetstone. She said she could not love a Yankee and she was not afraid to tell them so." The irrepressible Mollie Smith so impressed Mr. Meadows that he finished his report to the provost by saying "I think she is a bad rebel and a very great enemy of the Yankees and should be punished for her actions."[73]

By the time Mollie Smith's avowed dislike of Yankees got her on the provost's record the war was indeed over. Men were coming home from the army and there was the semblance of a return to civil life. Guerrillas, with the exception of the band led by Champ Ferguson, were allowed to surrender on the same terms as offered the major Confederate armies. John Cravens, assistant adjutant general for "Military Sub-District # 1,

Defenses of the N&C RR," wrote to Captain Henry Shook at McMinnville on May 19, 1865, saying that his report of receiving the surrender of numerous bands of bushwhackers had been approved by higher authority. The captain was authorized to continue accepting the surrender of all others who came in and was to send a list of those who had given up, along with a description of whose command they had been a part.[74]

This did not, however, mean a return to law and civility. Some of the guerrillas had simply become outlaws and they had no intention of readily returning to the ways of peace. Mrs. Martha Marshal was the victim of one such band.

> On Saturday the sixth day of May A.D. 1865 about one o'clock at night a party of four men rode up to my house in Franklin County Tenn. They came to the door and pushed said door open. Geo Pless who was then living there opened the door. They asked who lives here. He answered Pless. They then asked if this was the place Nelson was killed at. This Nelson was a Guerrilla Capt & killed my brother in law while surprised in robbing the house, some time previous. Pless answered them no sir this is not the place. The same man then came in and hitting Pless over the head forced him to sit down. They or two of them then commenced robbing the house. While the two were engaged in robbing the house one of the other two seized me and commenced taking liberties with my person. I broke way from him, and going to one of the others appealed to him to make the other stop which he did. They then dragged Mr. Pless into the floor and told him they were going to kill him that if he wanted to pray he must do so then. Mr. Pless got to his knees to pray just at that time I started to leave with my two little children just as I got to the door the one who was about to kill Mr Pless stepped to the door and told the two who were there to guard us and to see to it I did not get away. He then

took Mr Pless out of the house to kill him when the same man who made the one spoken of above leave me alone took him Pless from the other. Mr Pless succeeded in slipping off and affected his escape. Three of them then rode off leaving one of their party behind. The man left behind entered the house and catching Mrs Pless was about affecting his purpose on her person when she begged him to desist saying it would kill her since she was expecting every moment to be confined. He says then by G— D— I'll have that other woman and catching hold of my babe which I had in my arms threw it in the backside of the bed. He then caught holt of me & threw me up on the bed and threatened to kill me. I again jumped off when he caught both hands and forced me down in the bed striking me in the side with his fist or pistol he said G— D— you, you push me off & I will kill your baby. He succeeded in attaining his purposes. I with Mrs Pless & children left the house and went over to my fathers. While at my fathers the four again entered but left. While we were at the house the one who raped me there jumped on the bed for the purpose of burning the house. Mrs Pless extinguished it. Their brutality toward me was most inhumane. The whole party was very large but four entered the house. I did not recognize any of the parties.[75]

The problems with outlaws would not end rapidly because the Union troops were anxious to go home and civil law had not been reestablished in Tennessee. Actually, the return of civil law made the situation worse in some places since a county sheriff did not have the manpower available to a provost. Yet, peace of a sort had come and people wanted as much of a return to normal as they could achieve. Beginning with the smaller posts, then continuing with the larger posts along the main line of the railroad, the Union forces of occupation slowly withdrew and the provost marshal went with them.

McMinnville Tenn Warren County Sept 6, 1865

We the undersigned Loyal Citizens of Warren County would respectfully represent that peace and harmony now prevail throughout this section of the country.

County offices have been qualified and courts established throughout the district, and the civil machinery of the government put in operation. It is our belief that civil authority is amply sufficient without the assistance of the military to enforce the laws and preserve good order in this community.

Therefore we respectfully request that troops be withdrawn from this place.

A total of 52 signatures appear on the document.

Murfreesboro Sept 22, 1865

Reply returned. The troops were removed from McMinnville to Carthage about 10 days since. R.W. Johnson Bvt Maj Genl[76]

Although Tennessee would not be readmitted to the Union and full civil law restored until 1868 the final frenzy was over.

"When they came and took away my husband and sons— I have not seen them again—I knew many of them for they were my neighbors. When they came to burn our house I knew many of them for they were my neighbors. How can we ever be neighbors again?" These words are those of an Albanian woman interviewed on National Public Radio in August 1999 during the strife and ethnic cleansing in the Balkans. They could have been spoken by many in Middle Tennessee in 1865. Out of the fury and violence of occupation came the bitterness of Reconstruction.

4

The Unknown Warriors

    The role of African Americans in the American Civil War has been a matter of study ever since the war ended. Most study has focused on those who enlisted in the ranks of the Union army, although a small, but growing, body of research deals with those who cast their lot with the Confederacy. The provost marshal records reveal a new role for African Americans, that of army employees who aided the war effort without enlisting in the ranks, and those who kept family and community life as intact as possible in the midst of the whirlwind of war. Of course, some fell into a life of crime in the absence of the restraints of civil life while others found their circumstances had not changed a great deal even though they were now free instead of enslaved. It is a truism to say that the Civil War was a social revolution in the matter of race relations in the United States, but the provost marshal records reveal much never before known facts about the unknown warriors—men, women, and children who fought this unknown struggle in this unknown war.

    As soon as the Union army entered Middle Tennessee, during the Tullahoma campaign, black men and women came flocking into their camps. Many of these found freedom through employment with the occupying forces. As skilled teamsters, cooks, and as unskilled laborers loading and unloading wagons and railroad cars, these people could make an immediate contribution to the Union war effort. For that reason, many commanders who used their labor opposed the recruiting of their laborers into the ranks of the army. It would take months of training to produce a good soldier, but a good wagon driver was already at hand—why make the change? This attitude is seen in a report filed from Pocahontas, Tennessee, in late June 1863, even before the Tullahoma campaign was finished.

> Col. Aug. Mersy, Comdg 2d Brigade
>   The following is a list of Contrabands who have been employed in the Quartermaster Department by Lt. S.E. Adams AAQm. They drew the amount of clothing attached to their names and on yesterday (June 28, 1863) they were enticed away by a Colored Sergt called Webb to join the 2nd Alabama Regiment.

Name	Amount of Clothing Drawn		
Warren Hill	1 shirt 1 pr socks 1 pr shoes 1 blouse		
Jackson Foot	Andy Ayres		
Sampson Harbin	Dany Moon	Tom Frazier	
Andy Spell	Fitz Parmer	Isaac Connsel	

> Total drawn 8 shirts, 7 pr socks, 8 pr shoes, 3 blouses
> I understand that the colored Segt is here at present trying to lure others away.
>   Respectfully, S.E. Adams, 1st Lt AAQM 2d Brigade[1]

In addition to the lieutenant being upset over the loss of good workers, and being unhappy over the inevitable paperwork the lost clothing would entail, there is another issue at work here. The Army of the Cumberland was largely made up of Midwesterners. These men were strongly committed to preserving the Union but had equally strong reservations about racial equality. The states of Iowa, Illinois, and Indiana all had provisions in their state constitutions and laws banning Negro residents within their state borders. No Midwestern state gave civil rights to free Negroes at any time during the Civil War and there was strong postwar opposition to the 14th and 15th Amendments to the U.S. Constitution granting equal rights. At no time did the Army of the Cumberland use Negro troops in a combat role, and black units in rear areas were strictly segregated from the rest of the army. In short, this report shows opposition to making African Americans combat soldiers. Wagon drivers were inferior in standing in the army, but soldiers could claim equality with each other.

Lieutenant Adams was still at Pocahontas at the end of July and he filed another report of the list of persons hired by him at that village. This report is interesting because it gives the occupation of the former slaves, and shows their wages.

> Report of Persons and articles employed and hired at Pocahontas Tenn during the month of July 1863 by Lieut S.E. Adams, AAQM

Thomas Hooker	Laborer	$10 per month
Edgar Madlock	Laborer	$10
Henry Madlock	Laborer	$10
Charles Ray	Laborer	$10
Geo McGuff Ray	Laborer	$10
Willis Ray	Laborer	$10
Robert Ray	Laborer	$10
Philip Davy	Laborer	$10
John Alexander	Laborer	$10
Eva Ray	Cooks for Qm Employees	$5
Margaret Ray	Cooks for Teamsters	$5
Harriet Cole	Cooks for contrabands	$5
Clemain Cole	Cooks for Teamsters	$5[2]

On August 7, 1863, extensive lists of employees were turned in to the provost marshal. One hundred eighty-three names are found on the various lists, including the name of "Jacob Shanders, a free negro from Indiana, employed by Capt. Bedford, 15th Indiana, as a servant."[3] Many of the employees are listed only by a first name and, in some cases where the servants are children, one suspects the names were only recently given. There are an unusual number of children listed as "Abe" or "Rosy" (apparently in honor of General Rosecrans). While the occupation of "teamster" and "cook" is the most frequent, there are numerous "Servants" hired by officers and even by the wives of officers. Not all the workers appear to have been serving for wages or to have been doing so of their own volition.

In March 1864, one young Negro man asked for a pass to go from Nashville back to his home near McMinnville. He had been forced to leave his wife and family to drive stock from Warren County to Nashville in 1863 when the Union army entered the area. Since going to Nashville he had not been allowed to return to his home. To this young man, working for the Union army must have seemed very much like slavery. He was forced to leave his wife and family, had to go far away to a place from which he was not permitted to return, and received only food, clothing, and shelter in exchange for his labor. Now his wife and family were hungry because the Union army had taken away from the plantation all the men, leaving the slave owner 25 women and children who could not produce their own food and whom the owner could not feed.[4] The nation had a long way to go to make freedom more than a word.

Many African American men did desire to be soldiers and, after the Emancipation Proclamation went into effect on January 1, 1863, the government of the United States was anxious to recruit them, albeit they would serve in segregated units. Special officers were used to recruit black men and they often found their life to be anything but easy. One recruiting officer, W. F. Wheeler, claimed "heavy expenses" since he had to replace equipment lost to a Confederate cavalry raid. He also found the country not to be safely under Union control.

Samuel Mitchell & John Buchanan (colored) who were sent to Winchester found it unwise to go farther than

Decherd. They reported to me yesterday with several men and I ordered them to continue on and report to Mr Moore and have the men enlisted, as I had no accommodation for them here, everything being occupied by the military. I have three men out, one gone into Lincoln Co — but I hardly think he will be able to get there on act of "bush-whackers" — one in Coffee Co — and the other into Marshal Co. They are to report Sunday if successful. Little can be done here in town. The weather has been & is very bad, nothing could be done outside. The men who go out are very much in want of revolvers and ask if I cant procure some for their use. I miss my own, lost during the late "raid," very much. Cant it be replaced at Uncle Sam's expense? Also one or two for use of men.[5]

Wheeler was not the only person engaged in the recruiting business. Recruiting agent S. H. Chase received $221.20 for "expenses" involved in recruiting in the Month of February, 1864.[6] This was a very lucrative business indeed — for the recruiters!

There is one aspect of the recruitment of "Colored Troops" not much discussed. It was possible for slave owners who were loyal to the Union to send their slaves into the army and to receive payment for them. This practice appears to have been widespread and was encouraged by recruiting agents as it allowed them to fill their quota of recruits with a minimum of effort. W. F. Wheeler commented on this practice in a report from Wartrace in October 1863: "I have sent off all my men some five in number. They return Sunday when I expect to send you a squad. A Mr Eulis has just been inquiring after his boy, one Jas Eulis. I enlisted him. Will you see if he is at Camp and passed an examination? So I can give the man a rect for him. Let me know by return mail. Also see about Wm Houston if he passed also."[7]

The same sort of query came from Scottsboro, Alabama, in February 1864; only on this occasion the slave owner, A. J.

Huggins, directly approached a Union recruiting officer to inquire if he could enroll his slaves. Other slave owners were interested in doing the same thing, according to Huggins.

> I write you on behalf of myself and others in regard to the Colored population of North Ala. Many of us have slaves and wish to turn them over to the Govt to be used as may be deemed necessary, but there appears to be no provision for that purpose in Ala, it is true there is a recruitment station at Stevenson but the authorities there will not receive them unless the Slave is willing to enlist which few prefer to do, but will leave home, go into camps and consume the ration of the soldier in an act of little benefit. We wish to do what is required if we knew how. I will ask a question before closing. If our slaves go away into camps before there is any regular provision for turning them over to the government will the owner be entitled to receive all the benefits he would have done provided he had delivered them in person to the recruitment office? I make inquiry in regards to col'd women as well as men.[8]

General Lovell Rousseau commented that disorder and confusion were being created by the habit of "Officers in command of colored troops pressing all able-bodied slaves into the military service of the United States. One communication from citizens near McMinnville I have already forwarded you. Many similar complaints have been made. Forced enlistments I have endeavored to stop but find it difficult if not impracticable to do so."[9] These provost documents make it necessary to reevaluate the usual picture of black men eagerly seeking blue uniforms and taking up muskets to gain their freedom. The policy of the United States government was not entirely free of the concept of forced labor and unwilling servitude. There were approximately 180,000 African Americans in the Union forces. The question must now be asked, how many of them went there willingly? How many were sent to the army by slave owners eager to protect a financial investment which they were about to lose? Since the Emancipation Proclamation had no legal merit, and since Lincoln was anxious not to alienate pro-Union slave owners, the practice of forced recruitment of slaves by the army was quite feasible.

Newly found freedom was not always well used, and in all cases the new status required adjustments in actions and attitudes. On January 30, 1864, Major General Lovell Rousseau, in command of the Department of the Cumberland, commented in an official report:

> The negro population is giving much trouble to the military, as well as to the people. Slavery is virtually dead in Tennessee, although the State is excepted from the emancipation proclamation. Negroes leave their homes and stroll over the country uncontrolled. Hundreds of them are supported by the Government who neither work nor are able to work. Many straggling negroes have arms obtained from soldiers, and by their insolence and threats greatly alarm and intimidate white families, who are not allowed to keep arms, or who would generally be afraid to use if they had them. The military cannot look after these things through the country, and there are no civil authorities to do it.
>
> In many cases Negroes leave their homes to work for themselves, boarding and lodging with their masters, defiantly asserting their right to do it. It is now and has been for some time the practice of soldiers to go to the country and bring in wagon-loads of negro women and children to this city, and I suppose to other posts. Protections are granted to some slaves to remain with their owners, exempt from labor . . . General Payne has adopted the policy of hiring slaves to their owners by printed contracts, made in blank and filled up for the occasion, which, though a flagrant usurpation, I have not

interfered with his action on that and many other sub-
jects, preferring to submit such matters to the consideration of the general commanding.[10]

The "General Payne" mentioned by Rousseau was Eleazer
Paine who also made a reputation under Milroy for his blood-
thirsty attitude toward Confederate sympathizers.

In the absence of the old restraints of master-slave rela-
tionships, some turned to the Union army for help in controlling their former property, or in seeking protection from the
acts of the Freedmen. Alexander Hodge of Bedford County
contacted General Milroy to ask for help controlling his slave,
Jim. He said, "My negro man Jim Hodge came to my house
and cut up at a desperate rate, disputed my word five or six
times, drew a little wagon tongue to strike me with & said he
asked me no odds and that he would have my hill cleaned up
in less than three days. I would like to have him arrested and
carried to Nashville and put in the service of the Government
or deal with him as you see proper."[11] Alexander Hodge convinced the provost marshal he was a "Loyal Citizen." That
both master and slave had the same last name seems odd at
first but it is quite common to find in the provost records that
slaves had no surname but took, or were given, that of their
owner.

In other cases the army had to resort to courts-martial to
keep freed slaves within the bounds of the law. Such a court
was convened in Lincoln County in May 1865, to try Robert
Neaven, an African American, who had gone on a limited crime
spree. William Dyer was president of the court[12] which tried
Neaven for breaking into the smokehouse of John Roach and
taking 16 gallons of whiskey. Later that same day Neaven stole
27 yards of cloth from Clemy Woodword. Found guilty of both
charges, Neaven was sent as a prisoner to the stockade in
Tullahoma.[13]

One other case is suggestive since it indicates gang activity on the part of an integrated group which included recently

freed slaves. While bushwhackers often turned into robbers, this is the only group found which included both whites and blacks.

B. F. Sanders being duly sworn deposes and says:

I reside in Franklin County Tenn over twelve months since my family and myself were sick with small pox and my son-in-law Larkin Smith lived on my land on a certain day I heard my daughter hallo for me and started to her house before I reached the house I was met by a shower of rocks I went on and seen ten or twelve men among whom I recognized Ki Hall, Marshall Simmons, Huskins, Gilbert Runnels, Wade Sanders, Wm Gibson & Dick Jones they were in the yard when I reached the crowd I enquired what was the matter some one replied that Smith had been stealing I observed Ki Hall to be the one who threw most of the Rocks after a time Hall started away and I made the remark there is the man who threw the rocks the crowd started as it were in that direction and I went with them Hall came back to the crowd and got a gun from Jones and came up to within seven feet of me and shot me. I was taken into Smiths house and from there taken home the next day the following day my daughters house was burned by as I believe these same men as some of them came to my house. Two days after this Pink Brannon colored came to my house and wanted to buy my blacksmith tools. I would not sell them to him he then remarked that I had best sell them as they would be on hand to burn my house in a short while. After some further conversation he left and some time afterwards a party of men came to my house and Pink Brannon and the Capt of the Band (Temp) came into the house. The negro remarking they have come to burn your house and I had better let him have the tools we had some further conversation about the tools but finally the party left without burning my house. The following day the negro Pink Brannon came back and tried to prevail on me to let him have the tools but I refused upon this he went to where I had the tools and loaded them into the wagon stating I didn't made a d — —d bit of difference he would have them any how he then came into the house and Temp counted out seventy five dollars in Confederate money and gave it to my daughter at this time Temp was with him. They left my premises taking the tools with them

B.F. Sanders X his mark[14]

Boone Sanders, brother of B. F. Sanders, supported the testimony already given in the case, adding that a fire had actually been built under the house in which his brother was bedridden. Boone Sanders added that Pink Brannon was offering to sell the tools back to B. F. Sanders for a price of $50 in U.S. currency.[15] Mary Sanders, daughter of B. F. Sanders, corroborated his testimony and added that the tools were worth $75.[16]

Given the rapid transformation of their lives from slavery to freedom, from tight constraints to no bounds at all, it is no wonder that some members of the black community used their new freedom to get revenge or to copy the lawless ways they saw so many of the white community following. Some, however, merely tried to make a living. This was the case with the former slaves of Gabriel Maupin of Bedford County. They appealed to General George Thomas at Nashville, saying that

they were the slaves of one Gabriel Mopping who resided on his plantation near Shelbyville Bedford County known as the "Mopping Place" until after the battle of Murfreesboro at which time he ran down South with General Bragg's Army and has not since returned. That he has abandoned his said plantation.

Petitioners wish further to represent that after the said Gabriel Mopping ran South and abandoned his said plantation they had no place to stay at except on said plantation and they stayed there and worked and made a support for themselves until one Doctor Saml Whitson took possession of said plantation and ordered off petitioners and they are now turned out of their home and have no place to stay at or no means of making a support.

Petitioners would further state that although their old Master the said Gabriel Mopping was a very great Rebel and aided and assisted and sympathized with the so called Confederacy yet when he was about to leave he requested and desired his Slaves petitioners to stay on the plantation and work it and try and support themselves. Which they have done until turned out by said Doctor Saml Whitson.

In view of the premises the said petitioners would ask and request of the Maj Genl Commanding the Department of the Cumberland to order that petitioners be permitted to reside on the abandoned plantation of their former master and that said Doctor Saml Whitson be prohibited from turning them off said plantation they have no home no shelter no place to go and no means of making a living and therefore rely on the action of the Maj General as their only hope as he is the only person who can under the peculiar circumstances grant recourse.

Andrew Mopping X his mark Abner Mopping X his mark
Ben Mopping X his mark

J. P. Dillon, assistant special agent in the Treasury Department, was asked to determine if Maupin's land had been seized by the U.S. Treasury Department under the Confiscation Act which allowed the U.S. Government to strip Confederate sympathizers of their property. Dillon replied that the property had not been seized.[17] An investigation was then undertaken by Dillon who duly reported that Gabriel Maupin had voluntarily abandoned his Bedford County property and that the farm was now in the possession of Doctor Samuel Whitson who had tried to move the former Maupin slaves off the land. In this report Treasury Agent Dillon directed Captain Charles Thayer to

> proceed to the Town of Shelbyville, Tenn and in case the facts are as stated, inform the present occupant that he must forthwith surrender said farm with all stock and farming utensils that was found upon said place by him, and to insure that this order is carried out, no description of property shall be taken from said place until a thorough investigation as to ownership can be had.
>
> You will also restore to their home the former slaves of said Mopping. But said farm will be leased to them under instructions which will hereafter be given.[18]

Despite the best efforts of the army, the Treasury Department, the Freedmen's Bureau, and other agencies, the former slaves were often taken advantage of by those who wanted their work and then were unwilling, or unable, to pay for services received. First Lieutenant Samuel Davis, provost marshal at Shelbyville, reported that "Jeannie (colored girl)" had been driven away from her place of work by her mistress, Mrs. Polly Wells. Jeannie was not allowed to take her clothes with her when she was forced to leave. The lieutenant asked the provost at Fayetteville, Captain C. H. Haverly, to "send, if practical, some of your men to her residence and get the things mentioned and have them taken to Fayetteville where the girl can get them."[19]

From Nashville, a request was sent to the provost at McMinnville on behalf of Caroline Price, a freed slave. Caroline had a daughter named Martha, about 14 years old, who resided with one John French at or near McMinnville. Caroline had made frequent attempts to obtain possession of her child, and the daughter had made repeated efforts to come to this city to reside with her mother, but "these endeavors have in each instance been foiled & prevented by the said French, with the aid & connivance of the commander of the Post of McMinnville, French being (or reported to be) disloyal."[20]

At Shelbyville the provost was ordered to help "Serena, a colored woman," reclaim her personal property from Washington Goodwin. The attempt failed, however, because Goodwin had moved to Cincinnati, Ohio, and had sold Serena's property to a Union soldier before he left. [21]

Ganch Daily, "a black man living 18 miles from Tullahoma, on the Mulberry Pike" reported that he was robbed of 14 sides of bacon by a party of guards accompanying a Union wagon train. He said the men who took his meat were all mounted and left their post with the wagons to come to his house. General Milroy ordered an investigation of the event and directed that Daily was to receive back the meat or be paid the value of the same. [22]

At about the same time George William Henry, listed as "Colored," complained that he had gone to the house of Mr. Charles Cannon of Bedford County to get some clothes which belonged to his wife. Mr. Cannon had previously "driven away" his wife. Cannon refused to turn over the clothes to Henry, saying that "someone else would have to come to get them." Henry further stated that his wife had been beaten when driven away from the Cannon house and that he had been threatened with shooting if he brought up the subject of the clothes again. Moreover, Cannon had expressed contempt for General Milroy.[23] The same week, Ann Crowell got an order from the provost allowing her to remove her child from the farm of James Newton of Bedford County and to move to Murfreesboro.[24]

The Union army came in for some complaints from the ex-slaves. Adeline Blackwell of Franklin County had agreed to cook for Battery M of the 2nd Missouri Light Artillery. In March 1865 she complained that she had been cooking for the unit since the previous December but that the commanding officer, Lieutenant Flag, had never paid her even though she had asked for her pay a number of times. She wanted $20 for January and February before she continued to cook for the rest of the month of March.[25]

Occasionally a case arose where a child who had been a slave had bonded with the slave owner and did not want to establish ties with a parent the child had scarcely known. Mrs. R. Hesay of Coffee County was threatened with punishment by General Milroy if she did not turn over to Harriet Selman her two children. Mr. R. A. Mathews replied that he thought the letter was addressed to him since he had one of the children but did not have the other.

> I would further add the child I have was given me by its former owner Mrs Mathews to support. This was about six years since the child being four years old. The other child spoken of was given to Mrs Mathews daughter who is living some seventy five miles from me. The within order was given me by the mother of the children she remarking that I had to get her the other chile (sic) which I never had in my possession. I am willing to give up the child I have if so ordered but when I told him to go with his mother he positively refused and ran off. The child expresses and has expressed the uttermost opposition to going or being with his mother. All of which is most respectfully submitted.[26]

Near Hillsboro a farmer named C. F. Herd wrote to General Milroy that he needed help in evicting "the colored man Ben Patton now living on the Patterson Place." Herd had seized the Patterson farm to satisfy a debt and found Patton living there even though he was not, and never had been, a slave of Patterson. Since he was not associated with the farm while a slave, Patton had no legal claim to live on the land at the present. Patton had not only refused to leave the land, he refused to pay rent. Captain Roberts of the Hillsboro Home

Guard was ordered by Milroy to look into the matter. Roberts was able to reply that Herd and Patton had settled the matter between themselves out of court.[27] It seems that a familiar pattern was emerging. Land owners needed labor; laborers needed a place to work. Self-interest on both parts brought resolution to disagreements.

Some cases which came before the authorities may have been the result of bad temper or of drunkenness. Eli Hill of Fayetteville was charged on March 21, 1865, accused of "with force of arms unlawfully and violently seize the person of one Jesse Whittaker, a peaceable colored citizen of said Fayetteville, Tennessee, and did knock down, whip, and otherwise maltreat said Whittaker to the great injury of his person."[28]

Greed was always a problem when the seemingly defenseless Freedmen possessed goods which a more powerful person desired. Lieutenant G. W. Glynn, 102nd New York, has already been mentioned in the case of the looting of the house of Mrs. Gail Hibbs. On March 31, 1865, he was the subject of another complaint when Henry Taylor testified:

> I reside in Winchester, Franklin Co Tenn and formally belonged to Mr Henry Taylor a resident of said county. Sometime in Feby last Lt Glynn and Dr Devers came to my house and demanded of me my horse. I told them I bought the horse and paid for him and had a right to keep him. Mr March and Mr John Brandon were present at the time and informed Glynn that he was not a government horse, that he belonged to me and that they had no right to take him. Glynn then stated that he would take the horse to Tullahoma and see if he belonged to the Government that if he was not a Govt horse he would return him to me the next morning. I have learned since that Glynn never took him to Tullahoma but some time after traded him off to Thomas Aldridge for another horse. I respectfully ask that some means be taken to restore to me my property.[29]

On other occasions the sense of justice of the former slave demanded repatriations for work done as a slave. It is also obvious that owners changed their attitudes when a slave left with the Union army and then returned, having found that the Union army could not and would not support them for an indefinite period of time. The old master-slave relationship had disappeared and nothing had yet developed to take its place. A woman identified only as "Amer-colored" is one such case.

> I have lived with Thomas Dean citizen of Bedford County Tenn I am about forty seven (47) years of age I have been his slave for this number of years have worked in the fields plowed etc. I was told to leave last Sunday evening he gave as a reason that he did not want any niggers about him who left with the Yankees and came back again he informed me that he would pay me well for last years work all that I have received from him is seven dollars and two hogs. I have four children living. He has sent me out in the world without any means of making a livelihood. I am procuring something to eat any place I can. I expect the Military authorities to force this man to do me justice after these long years of labor.[30]

It should be noted that the phrase "lived with" did not have any sexual connotation in the 19th century. It was a synonym for "lived on the farm of."

More often than reparations for slavery the issue was clearly one of personal property. Mr. John Dyer of Shelbyville was ordered to bring to the Provost Office all the bedding, clothes, and personal belongings of Amy Greer, who had been his slave and who was moving elsewhere.[31]

Eliza Moore wished to move from Shelbyville to Tullahoma and paid Mr. Jack Ivy to haul her clothing, books, men's clothing, dishes, knives, and forks in his wagon to that place for her. The goods never arrived and after repeated attempts to have them delivered, Eliza Moore found that Ivy had moved and had taken the goods with him.[32] This is an interesting case in that a former slave lists "books" as being among her personal property.

George Solomon of Shelbyville owned a house occupied by "Harriet Story — colored." He found the real estate was more valuable than the house standing on it and decided to build a new structure on the property. Harriet Story, however, refused to vacate the house. On April 30, 1865, three members of the 42nd Missouri, William Buckmaster, George Chapman, and Thomas Adams, talked with Solomon and then went to the house of Harriet Story. There the men took whatever tools they could find and proceeded to rip a small room away from the main room of the building. When Story, who was visiting next door, heard the noise of her house being demolished she ran over to investigate, only to be driven off by rocks thrown at her. She appealed to the provost for help.[33]

On occasion it seems some of the ex-slaves tried to play on the sympathy of the Union army courts to get money they were not owed. Charley Winton appears to have been in this situation. Charley sued his former owner, John Winton, aged 80, for money Charley said was owed him. He claimed:

> I have been working for John Winton who resides in Warren County between McMinnville and Hillsboro since I became twenty one years of age as near as I can recollect about fifteen years since I was hired out by John Winton to another man and remained with him about four years this man is Thomas Mitchell. While with Mitchell I saved some money which I made by extra labor. After I returned to Winton some eight or ten years since He was in need of money and requested me to lend him some. I loaned him fifty dollars in silver and fifty dollars in bank notes and he promised to pay me the money back with interest. I worked for him up to about five months since when he drove me away from his house

stating he did not want me and that I would have to do for myself being a cripple. I have been living with my half sister since that time. Some few weeks since I went to Mr Winton and asked him for my money and the interest he refused to pay me either the principal or the interest and said he would shoot me if I ask for it again. The claim was sent to Captain S.H. Charles of the Hickory Creek Home Guards for settlement.

Problems arose for Charley when his own mother, Aggie Winton, swore the amount loaned had been $10. His brother, Nat Winton, agreed with his mother on the amount. Neighbors of John Winton swore he was an honest man while one of Charley's friends said Charley could not be believed even when he was under oath. After listening to all sides of the question the court ruled John Winton should pay Charley $10 for clothes, hats, and shoes he deserved from his years of service but that no other money was due. General Milroy disapproved the verdict, however, and ordered interest paid on the $10.[34] Milroy took a very precise attitude in demanding every penny owed by slave owners should be paid to former slaves.

Jane King was a former slave of William King of Warren County. She complained to the provost that "On Monday evening last Miss Laura A. King, his sister, told me and the rest of the colored people that we would have to leave if we was free negroes and would have to go to Milroy and let him maintain us. I left the next morning and on the way I met Wm. King. He inquired where I was going. I replied Tullahoma to arrange business and would be back on Friday. He stated he would have the matter arranged by that time."[35] King agreed to give his workers half the crop for that year since they had commenced to make the crop when they were ordered to leave. Something of the same was experienced by Charles Cornelius. Cornelius swore that he had been hired by Robert Dwiggins to work on his farm at the rate of $15 per month. After several months of farm work Dwiggins asked Cornelius to work on a mill, work which Cornelius did not want to do. After seven months Cornelius was fired but he had received only $32 worth of clothing and $7 in cash. To support his claim Cornelius got testimony from a fellow worker, Wiley Sutton, who gave his deposition that Cornelius had done good work but did not want to work on the mill and that he had been forced to leave without being paid.[36]

With the war over, there was a demand for wood with which to rebuild the railroads and structures along its course. The provost records not only indicate a good deal of virgin timber still standing in Middle Tennessee, but show that those skilled in cutting and shaping that timber were in demand, even if their treatment was not always fair. James Hodges complained:

> I have been at work for Middleton Hollins a citizen of Bedford Co Tenn since the last of Aug 1864. I commenced by cooking for him which I did for a month for this he was to pay me $1.50 per day. The next month I was engaged in hewing cross ties for which I was to receive $2.00 per day. Another month at hewing trestle timbers Hollins agreeing to pay me $2.50 per day. The next three months he engaged me to hew ties and trestle timber, for hewing trestle timber he was to pay $2.50 per day & for ties $2.00 per day I worked about half the time hewing trestle timbers and half hewing ties. My boy worked for Hollins four months for which he agreed to pay him one dollar per day. In making this statement I have not reckoned in a month which we both lost. On a settlement with Hollins he paid me but $63.00 he said I had drawn $100.00 worth of rations which covered the whole amount. This was not true as I had drawn $10.00 worth. In another bargain he hired me to furnish him with 20 sticks of timber 21 ft long 8 by 10 inches sq for which he agreed to pay me $50.00. I furnished the timber but Hollins refused to pay me. I then furnished him with

twenty-five sticks of timber 16 ft long & 8 by 10 inches square for which he agreed to pay me $16.00 but failed to do so. I then furnished him with five sticks of timber 25 ft long 8 by 10 inches square five sticks more than eighteen ft long 10 inches square another five sticks twenty one ft long 10 inches sq. 1 stick twenty seven ft long 10 in sq. There was to have been five sticks of the last but the timber ran out. Hollins owed him Hodge twenty four dollars & Mary Hodge $16.00 for cooking. Hollins hired another of his boys at $1.00 per week his work amounting to $10.00 Hollins owed me $2.00 more for bottoming chairs and $2.00 for making a rack besides $10.00 in money which I lent him. William Jolly was my boss during the time I worked for Hodge owed me $8.50.[37]

John Douglas, captain of the Home Guards for the 2nd District of Bedford County, felt that A. G. Ball was getting a bad deal in a case brought against him. Ball was in jail at Tullahoma, accused by a black couple identified only as Isaac and Fanny, of stealing money from them. Douglas said Isaac and Fanny had been troublemakers for the last 25 years, often accusing people of stealing from them. In the case of Ball, the amount allegedly stolen had been variously stated as $30, $60, and $80. It appeared that Isaac and Fanny had brought the charge at the instigation of "an old ignorant woman, a pretended fortune teller residing at Wartrace." Douglas then "respectfully request as a favor that Ball be allowed to return and be tried by the company court of this district, the 2d, it is composed of five men of undoubted loyalty, good moral character and strict honesty and integrity, whose oath or word would be taken before any court of justice." Ball was quite willing to post bond, so the case was sent to the Home Guard court for trial.[38]

Freedom meant hard times, as it turned out. Those who had worked on land as slaves did not have any legal claim for compensation for those years of labor and had to try to begin life with no resources except the clothes they wore. In some cases, they had no option except to return to the very place where they had been held as slaves and to try to bargain with the very people who had held them in bondage. Sometimes the former slave master did not want to deal with his former property and there was nothing left to do but throw oneself on the mercy of strangers. The promises which some of the more radical of the abolitionists had held out concerning "forty acres and a mule" proved to be empty when a more moderate government leadership refused to confiscate the land of Confederates to give to the slaves. The unreasonably high expectations of some former slaves and the intransigent attitude of some former slave owners did nothing to provide a good basis on which to build smoothly functioning race relations in the years following the war.

Perhaps the biggest surprise facing the freedmen was the attitude of many members of the Union army. Some of those who refused to pay wages due were Union soldiers who duped black men and women into working for them for nothing. More shocking were those cases in which the Northern authorities sided with ex-Confederate land owners to insure that former slaves continued to be docile laborers. In the area around the N&C Railroad, the most notorious case involved the Bonner family of Fayetteville, Tennessee. Dr. William Bonner was a medical doctor who invested in land in the Elk River bottoms near Fayetteville. During the war he continued to raise cotton on this land and managed to sell some of his crop at a very favorable price since the fiber was in short supply and great demand in the North. As a well-known rebel sympathizer Dr. Bonner was often called on by the Federal authorities to supply food for fellow Confederates held prisoner in the local jail. At the end of the war William Bonner, Jr., returned home from four years in the Confederate cavalry. Managing the family plantations, he soon found himself involved with the occupying authorities. Brevet Brigadier General S. A. M. Dudley was furious over Bonner's actions in regard to his workers and filed a report, accompanied by testimony, which documented the cause for his anger. The general said:

> Herewith I have the honor to forward charges against William Bonner for now a citizen planter, formerly a Rebel Officer residing near Fayetteville Lincoln County Tenn together with bond marked "A" his own statement of the brutal transaction marked "C" made in the presence of the parties whose names are attached and the statement of Private Matthew Mullins and Tyler Harrison 5th Tenn Cavalry marked "B" and "D" the latter under oath. I think this affair one of the most shameful unwarranted and cruel of its kind that has taken place during my service in this section of Tennessee. I think there is sufficient evidence to prove that Capt Shipp did order the men Mullins and Harrison to proceed with Bonner and Capt Askins to the plantation with the intention of having the negro man Henry, whipped, certain it is that he sanctioned it as he took no steps to arrest the party until a letter promising to attend to his (Henry's) case again, when the outrage of the day before was reported to him.
>
> If United States soldiers wearing the uniform of such cannot find other occupation than that of being hired out to whip the negroes of returned Rebel Officers, I think the sooner they are disbanded the better for the honor of the service. I have relieved Capt Shipp from duty as Pro Mar at Fayetteville Tenn and ordered him in arrest. William Bonner Jr I have held to bail for appearance before Military Commission in the sum of three thousand dollars. Privates Mullins and Harrison are in the stockade awaiting trial. Charges will be forwarded tomorrow, the three Askins's, one a Captain of the Home Guard of Lincoln County I have sent for, they will be here tonight

and will go in the stockade to await trial. The negro boys back still exhibits a frightful sight. When he first reported on the 6th inst there were gashes on his person which would receive half a lead pencil without protruding above the surface. Wm. Boner Jr is a son of Dr Bonner one of the wealthiest men in Lincoln County. He offered me any amount of money to settle the case and let it drop. I respectfully request that this case may be immediately brought before the Military Commission now in session at this post as all the witnesses can be assembled on one day.

In his own behalf Bonner said:

My name is William Boner, I reside in Lincoln County near Fayetteville Tenn. I know the boy present — his name is Henry Bonner — he has been a slave in our family for fifteen (15) or twenty (20) years, at the present he is hireling to me. I have about twelve work hands on the place, my contract with him is, that at the end of the season, I was to leave the compensation to a committee of citizens, in case of disagreement, the matter was to be left to a Federal officer. The character of this man, has been that he was always a very sullen and contrary darkey. On the evening of the 3d of July I had a difficulty with a colored woman — Mary — — after this I went to the fields, and this darkey commenced talking about the difficulty. I told him to stay there and work. He was quite imprudent, said he would stay and leave when he wanted to. I told him if he was so imprudent to me and would quit when-ever he liked, that he should not stay there, he said in reply, that he would do as he pleased, that I could not make him leave — that if I felt like it, I had better undertake it. All the hands were present as he had said they were going to town. I went to town also. I saw Capt Shipp on the morning of the 4th of July at Fayetteville. I made a statement to Capt Shipp who is

the Provost Marshal of the place. Capt Shipp said he
would send a guard down there and have the thing corrected. he did send down two soldiers from the 5th Tenn
cavalry, I presume, one was named Harrison and I think
the other was named Mullins. These two soldiers went
to the plantation. I was with the, also, Capt Adkins of
the Home Guards with the Captains two brothers, Joe
and Jim, who belong to the Home Guards, besides another party unknown. I think his name is Hastings. We
arrived at the plantation about 7 o'clock in the evening
of the 4th. The whipping was then administered on this
boy by the Federal Soldiers and Capt Adkins (the back
of the boy was exhibited here) I call that very severe
whipping. I did not think he was whipped so bad, it was
dark, I could not see. I was armed, most of the party was
armed. I was a little excited at the time, I do not remember what I did say. I cannot say whether I said I would
blow his brains out or not. When I first went up to the
house the boy Henry was tied to a tree by his hands being fastened around the tree. I was present all the time. I
did not count the licks. I should think about one hundred, perhaps there was more, the switches used were
either elm or birch I think elm—I cannot tell how many
the men had in their hands at the time. They whipped
him twice. On my repeating the imprudence of the boy
Henry to Capt Shipp he told me that he would send some
men or Guards down to the plantation and have the boy
corrected or whipped, and he made the [word not read-
able] go down with me that evening. The boy did not
threaten my life or threaten me with violence, at all. The
trouble with the woman at which the Negro boy, Henry
took exception was as follows. She had been at the house
for an hour, nursing her baby. I told her it was too long,
she replied she would do as she pleased, her attitude
was defiant. I then struck her. I had my knife open when

the affair commenced. I shut it and struck her on the head with the handle of the knife and with my fist. I shut it and struck her with a rock. She then went on the field repeating that she would suckle her baby and work when she pleased.

I want to make the additional statement in justice to Capt Shipp. When I went to the field the boy Henry brought up the subject of my treatment of the Woman, Mary, of the previous evening in a very unbecoming manner. From his attitude and the presence of the other Negroes I saw from the facts before me that I had better go away and let the Negro alone. I went away in preference to involving myself in any serious difficulty with them in my interview with Capt Shipp the Provost Marshal I expressed these views. I thought the Negro a dangerous man.

One of the enlisted men involved in the affair gave his account of what had happened:

My name is Matthew Mullins I belong to company "C" 5th Tennessee Cavalry. On the 4th of July I was at Fayetteville in the evening of the 4th of July I went out to Wm. Bonners plantation in company with Tyler Harrison of my company and Wm. Bonner also a Capt of the Home Guard we were joined by two other men on reaching the house of Wm Bonner. The whole party proceeded to the negro quarters we took out one of the negro's and whipped him about three hundred yards from the quarters we tied him face to a tree and fastened his hands on the other side with a bridle rein. We whipped him with elm switches two in a bunch with spangles on them I can not tell how long the switches were. We did not count the blows but I think they could not exceed one hundred and fifty — the negro howled right much he did not curse any body while we were whipping him — we whipped him for saucing his master Wm. Bonner — we were sent out under the charge of the home guard captain and were told to do what he directed and he directed the party to whip the negro.

Capt Shipp ordered myself and private Harrison to report to the Capt of the Home Guard for this duty. Capt Shipp told us to go out with home guard Capt and settle a difficulty between Wm. Bonner and a negro I have known soldiers sent out before to settle difficulties where negros have been whipped by soldiers.

Before the whipping Wm. Bonner took us to his own house and gave us a supper tolerable nice one. He and his wife set down at the same table with us. After we got through the whippings he told us he was much obliged to us then I returned to camp about 4 1/2 mile from Bonners house — Wm Bonner and the soldiers were armed with loaded pistols. The negro did not use any disrespectful language to Wm. Bonner or any other person present in my presence at this or any previous time.[39]

Bonner was fined $50 over the whipping, but the result of the case was even greater for the Home Guards. General R. W. Johnson said, in a general order, "These Home Guards did all the 'Negro Whipping' in these neighborhoods. Considering their disloyal character I have issued an order disbanding all such forces, unless organized under authority by the governor."[40]

As was traditional in the South, any suggestion of assault, or even of threatening behavior, by a black man toward white women was sure to receive a quick and violent response. Even if a dispute began over something else, if women became involved the level of violence escalated quickly. The case of William Elkins and Ben Edens would be typical of many such cases. On May 25, 1865, the provost in Tullahoma, Major A. W. Billings, took up the case of Benjamin Edens, "a colored man, citizen of Wartrace," who had received a crippling gunshot wound at the hands of William Elkins of Wartrace.[41]

In the testimony given on March 23, 1865, "Ben" Edens said:

> I live near Wartrace Bedford Co Tenn on or about the 25th day of Nov 1864 I went to the house of Bill Elkins citizen of Wartrace to procure a Govt mule which I obtained leave to procure and work through the winter from Lt in charge of the block house near Wartrace. I told Elkins that I had come for my mule as I had tracked him to his house he remarked he had no mule and his colored men without making any remarks drew up a pistol and fired at me the ball taking effect in my head. I was then running and looking back. I saw four negroes with Elkins at the head mounted on horses the party got within ten yards of me when Elkins drew up a double barreled gun and discharged two loads at me the loads were of slugs one load took effect in my left arm near the elbow the other in the back of the head. I fell to the ground and remained perfectly still. They rode about me for a few minutes one of them remarked he's dead as hell. After they rode away I managed to get to my house some one hundred and fifty yards distant with the aid of my wife and boy. My arm has been amputated and is not thoroughly well yet. I am still suffering from the wounds in my head.[42]

However, when Edens repeated his testimony in court at Shelbyville on June 2, 1865, he made some significant additions. Edens noted, this time, that the mule was claimed by William Elkins as his property. In going to claim the mule Edens had been accompanied by another Negro man, Gabe Scruggs, who had been killed in the affair. Edens also named the Negro men who accompanied Elkins as James, Milton, Frank, and Elijah.[43] One of these men, Milton Cobb, gave testimony that Edens and Gabe Scruggs had come to the Elkins farm and had taken the mule, and that he and Elkins, with the others, were tracking the animal to reclaim it. Cobb also noted that Elkins said "He hated Union men, and wished many times in my presence that they were all dead. Elkins reputation in the neighborhood in which he lives is very bad. He was accused of claiming things that didn't belong to him."[44]

Thomas Caldwell, a noted Union supporter and attorney in Bedford County, wrote to General Milroy attempting to put the matter in the context of the society and mores of the times, as Caldwell understood them. He argued that "Our education and training in this county may not have been in strict accordance with the Ten Commandments but we have always held to the belief that any injury or insult to our wives and female relations, whether Black or White men was the aggressor, and public opinion has invariably justified such acts, the result has always been that men, however viscous they would have been, have been careful and our females were protected from insults and injury so against nature. Since this war has unsettled everything, lawless and bad men have disregarded age sex and many acts of outrage have been inflicted on the weak and unprotected." As Caldwell presented the issue, Edens and Scruggs had gone to Elkins' house and threatened violence to Mrs. Elkins and her daughter while her husband was absent. This triggered the affair.[45]

Mrs. Elkins gave her testimony that Edens had been threatening her. She said that Edens came to her house, "used abusive and threatening language toward the family saying 'he would be god damned if didn't land them all in hell before Saturday night.' This was the 28th of Nov 1864. On the next day he came again in company with Gabe Scruggs and said they 'would be god damned if they didn't take all the horses.'"[46]

Virginia, the daughter of William and Arcelia Elkins, verified her mother's account.[47] Martha, "a colored person" who had lived on the Elkins farm for two years, described the fight in much the same terms as Mrs. Elkins and Virginia.[48] Alexander Spire of Pennsylvania, who was living at Wartrace, testified he had had a confrontation with Edens himself. He swore that

On or about the 1st of June 1864 I went to the house of Ben Eaton (col'd) for the purpose of getting some clothing which had been sent there for washing. Edens presented his pistol and said if I made an attempt to get the clothing he would shoot me and threatened to do whether or not. I left him and made no further attempt to secure the clothes. During Sept 1864 Edens came to my house one mile east of Wartrace and asked to see my wife. I fold him my wife was sick and that he could not see her and left but returned in a few minutes and said "he would be damned if he didn't see her." I told him to leave the house that she would not see him when he repeated his intentions of doing so and exhibited a pistol when he spoke. I kicked him off the porch in front of the door.

I used no threats or abusive language on the first occasion of his drawing the pistol but simply stated I wanted the clothing before the presentation of the weapon.

Edens has the reputation of being a dangerous and dishonest man in the vicinity where he lives. I saw him frequently in the night during the autumn of '64.[49]

The clearest evidence that Elkins and his Negro workers all felt threatened by Edens and Scruggs was given by Asa Vaughn at whose house Scruggs was killed. He testified that

On or about the 28th of Nov 1864 William Elkins, who resides about one mile from my residence near Wartrace Tenn and Three negro men came to my residence in pursuit of a negro man named Gabe Scruggs who ran into my house to evade them. The negro Gabe Scruggs, went into the loft or upper part of the house to keep from his pursuers, Elkins and the negroes. Elkins told him to come down and said they intended to have him. The man refused to come out of the house and one of the negroes with Elkins got up to the gable of the house and cut or made a hole through for the purpose of shooting the negro Gabe Scruggs who then jumped down and ran out of doors. Elkins and the negroes pursued him around the house and I heard the report of fire arms twice and went round the house and saw the negro Gabe Scruggs lying on the ground dead. Just before Elkins came to my house in pursuit of the negro Gabe Scruggs who was killed I heard the report of fire arms a short distance from my residence and when Mr Elkins came up he said he had shot a negro named Benjamin Edens. During the conversation he also said if one shot did not kill another one would.[50]

The outcome of the case in a court of law, civil or military, might be in doubt, but one fact was clear. The doctor had to be paid. "To W.H. Samson M.D.To medical attention to shot gun wound & amputating arm & etc $50.00."[51]

One of the great needs among the newly freed African Americans was education. It had been illegal to teach a slave to read and write since the Nat Turner Rebellion in Southampton, Virginia, in the 1830s. Some slave owners violated that injunction, either out of a religious desire that their slaves should be able to read the Bible or out of self-interest in having literate cooks and house servants. But the vast majority of slaves, the "field hands," were illiterate. The Freedmen's Bureau and various Northern missionary agencies undertook to supply this need. Soon schools were being erected all over the South and "Yankee School Marms" were coming to teach in them. The fact that these schools were all black, coupled with the attitude of Northern teachers toward unrepentant ex-Confederates, made these ventures unpopular and their futures somewhat uncertain. This proved to be the case in Tullahoma.

The undersigned members of the Board of Mayor and Alderman of the Town of Tullahoma have the honor to present the following statement for your consideration and action.

That on the 11th inst the school house erected in this Town for the education of Freedmen was by some person or persons unknown set on fire and burned.

The members of said Board would further state that every effort has been made to ascertain who committed the act to the end that they might receive such punishment as the case deserves. We firmly believe and aver that the building was not fired by persons living within the limits of the corporation. In deed but one sentiment is expressed towards the perpetrators of an act so repugnant to the good sense, morals, and social status of the community and that is of universal execration.

So fearful were the citizens that the Military authorities might attach blame to them (not having a true statement of the facts laid before them) and being determined to use every effort to promote the welfare and prosperity of the whole people they raised by voluntary subscription sufficient funds to erect a building in lieu of the one burned. This was accomplished before any troops arrived here and before it was known any would be sent.

The members of said Board would submit, in behalf of themselves and Citizens of the Town & vicinity, that they have on all occasions whether in public or private, avoided committing any act or making any representations which would delay a hasty and perfect restoration of Tranquility & peace.

They feel that the garrisoning of troops in The Town is creating a false impression where the true state of the case is not fully understood and that their loyalty, integrity, and honor are compromised promised thereby.

Believing General, that misrepresentations have been made in relation to the matter, and that the order establishing a garrison at this point was issued through a misapprehension of facts the members of said Board of Mayor and Alderman deemed it their duty to present to you a full statement of all the facts in the business.

At a meeting of the board convened at their council room on the 29th Inst, they resolved to dispatch a member of said board to Nashville to lay the matter before you. The bearer here of Alderman R.P. Gannaway was duly selected to discharge said duty and to ask on behalf of said Board and citizens of the Town that the troops now quartered here be withdrawn, believing that the necessity does not and never did exist for their being ordered here.[52]

J. F. Thomas, member of the State House of Representatives, reinforced this statement in a letter to General Thomas in which he presented the whole affair as settled and the school replacement building as being well under way. The work did not proceed quickly enough to suit the commander of the troops sent to Tullahoma, however. In an order reminiscent of Milroy he said:

> The work of building the new school house for the freed men of this community is not going on as it should, in consequence of this fact it is hereby ordered that the wealthy citizens of the town subscribe a proper amount for the completion of the work already commenced. If this order is not complied with immediately I shall be under the necessity of arresting all the leading & wealthiest men of the place & compelling them to work under guard until the building is completed the proper size.
> James Henry Capt 16th USCT Comdg[53]

The fact that the garrison was made up of Negro soldiers of the U.S. Colored Troops and that such a peremptory order was issued by the commanding officer did nothing to create good will between the races. Within the next year Coffee County would see an outburst of activity by the Ku Klux Klan. This would be short-lived, however, and the area did not become one of the hotbeds of Klan activity.

Over the following years there was an out-migration of African American residents to Nashville and Chattanooga as agriculture declined in much of what had been Military Sub-District #1. This meant there would be limited racial conflict in the area, but blood feuds among white residents who had taken opposite sides plagued the district for 30 years. Some people, like Moses Pittman, who had informed on so many of their neighbors, found it wise to leave the state. Pittman moved to California, according to his descendants. Some families split, drifted apart, and to the present time use variant spellings of the family name to differentiate who was "Union" and who was "Confederate." Churches also divided, with congregations made up of Union supporters affiliating with the "Northern" branch of various denominations while Confederate groups remained "Southern" in membership.

The unknown war, on the unknown battlefield, was fought by many unknown warriors. In some of its aspects, that war is not over yet. Its shadows flicker in the setting sun, its voices lurk just below the surface of contemporary discourse. It was, after all, not so long ago, and modern people would do well to remember, and to learn to avoid, the depths to which our fore-bears descended.

Notes

INTRODUCTION

1. *Official Records of the War of the Rebellion,* ser. 2, vol. 5, p. 149. Hereinafter cited as *O.R.*

   General Orders #100 extends from p. 149 to p. 164. Following citations to General Orders #100 are made to specific paragraphs of the Order, found in the pages cited above.

2. *O.R.,* pars. 21–23.
3. Ibid., pars. 27–28.
4. Ibid., par. 38.
5. Ibid., pars. 44, 46.
6. Ibid., par. 54.
7. Ibid., par. 60.
8. Ibid., pars. 81–82.
9. Milroy to Mary, May 5, 1864. Milroy Letters. Author's collection. These letters are also available at www.cwrc.org.
10. Ibid., Sept. 18, 1864.
11. Ibid., Nov. 15, 1864.

CHAPTER 1: THE UNKNOWN BATTLEFIELD

1. Michael R. Bradley, *Tullahoma: The 1863 Campaign for the Control of Middle Tennessee* (Shippensburg, Pa.: Burd Street Press, 2000), pp. 90–91.
2. Union Provost Marshal (UPM), File of Two or More Citizens, Microfilm Collection (MC) 416, roll 94.
3. UPM, MC 416, roll 21.
4. *O.R.,* ser. 1, vol. 23, pt. 2, pp. 526–27.
5. UPM, MC 345, roll 200.
6. Ibid., roll 190.
7. UPM, MC 416, roll 94.
8. Union Provost Marshal (UPM), File of Individual Citizens, MC 345, roll 79; Ibid., roll 5.

Private Tull is buried in grave H-3059 at Stones River National Cemetery, Murfreesboro, Tennessee. Private Bault is buried in grave H-3060 in the same cemetery.

9. Milo M. Quaife, *From the Cannon's Mouth: The Civil War Letters of General Alpheus Williams* (Detroit: Wayne State University Press, 1959), pp. 264–65.

10. Quaife, *Cannon's Mouth*, pp. 266–67.

11. UPM, MC 345, roll 152.

12. Ibid.

13. For a discussion of the role of the Pioneer Brigade in the Army of the Cumberland in 1863 see Geoffrey Blakemeyer, "The Pioneer Brigade" at http://www.thecivilwargroup.com.

14. See Richard McMurry, *Atlanta, 1864*, chap. 7 and app. 3 for a full discussion of the role the W&A played in both Union and Confederate strategy. App. 3 also discusses the problems raised by making a cavalry raid on the N&C or the W&A using the troops of Bedford Forrest from Mississippi.

15. The following all give details of Forrest's Raid into Middle Tennessee in September 1864:

Andrew Nelson Lytle, *Bedford Forrest and His Critter Company*.

Thomas Jordan and J. P. Pryor, *The Campaigns of General Nathan Bedford Forrest*.

John Allan Wyeth, *That Devil Forrest*.

16. UPM, MC 345, roll 204.

17. Ibid., roll 291.

18. Ibid., roll 115.

19. Ibid., roll 134.

20. UPM, MC 416, roll 22.

21. UPM, MC 345, roll 93.

22. Ibid., roll 27.

Dr. James A. Blackmore (Aug. 28, 1800–June 1, 1863), a Sumner County medical doctor and member of the State Medical Society in 1830, was active in public affairs. He was elected mayor of Gallatin in 1831, assisted in staging a grand welcome home for returning volunteers from the Second Seminole War of 1836, and was a member of the board of trustees of Sumner Female Academy from 1836 to 1841. He was a strong advocate for bringing the route of the Louisville & Nashville Railroad through Sumner County and Gallatin and, with this done, he became a founder, principal shareholder, and member of the five-man board of directors of the Gallatin Cotton Manufactory. When gold was discovered in California, he helped organize a stock company to finance and share in the expected profits of the local mining group of Wilson, Love, and Company. This information courtesy of historian Walter Durham who writes extensively about Sumner County and Tennessee history.

23. UPM, MC 345, roll 135.

24. Ibid., roll 268.

25. Ibid., roll 182.

26. Ibid., roll 149.

27. *O.R.*, ser. 2., vol. 5, pp. 277–78; Ibid., p. 619 ff; Ibid., vol. 6, p. 150.

28. UPM, MC 345, roll 296.

29. Ibid., roll 270.

30. Ibid.

31. UPM, MC 416, roll 45.

32. UPM, MC 345, roll 185.

CHAPTER 2: AN UNKNOWN STRUGGLE

1. UPM, MC 345, roll 261.

2. *O.R.*, ser. 1, vol. 17, p. 594; Ibid., vol. 23, p. 548; Ibid., vol. 31, pt. 3, p. 573.

    When Captain Frank Gurley was captured in the fall of 1863 Hunter Brooke, the judge advocate for the Army of the Cumberland, claimed that Gurley did not have a Confederate Commission when McCook was killed in August 1862. Brooke wanted Gurley tried for murder. General Bedford Forrest sent a letter through the lines on Dec. 12, 1863, stating that Gurley had been in Confederate service since 1861 and had been under Forrest's command both before and after the death of General McCook. The case of Captain Gurley eventually claimed the attention of both the U.S. and the C.S. secretary of war.

    In December 1863, Captain Gurley was tried by a military commission at Nashville and was found guilty of murder. General George Thomas suggested a sentence of five years' imprisonment, but Judge Advocate Holt, who prosecuted Gurley at the trial, held out for the death penalty.

    Gurley was held in the state penitentiary at Nashville until the spring of 1865 when he was sent to Point Lookout POW camp in Maryland. Under an exchange agreement he was sent to City Point, Virginia, on May 25, 1865, and returned to North Alabama. On Sept. 6 Secretary of War Edwin Stanton ordered Gurley's re-arrest and execution. On Nov. 24, 1865, Gurley was apprehended and sent to General George Thomas in Nashville to be executed. However, President Andrew Johnson suspended the sentence on Nov. 28. Seventy-four Union residents of Huntsville, Alabama, petitioned the president on Gurley's behalf and he was finally released as an exchanged POW on Apr. 17, 1866.

    The *O.R.*, ser. 2, vols. 6 and 8 contain most of the information about Gurley.

3. UPM, MC 416, roll 22.

4. Ibid., roll 23.

5. UPM, MC 345, roll 79.

6. UPM, MC 416, roll 29.

7. Quaife, *From the Cannon's Mouth*, pp. 6–9.

8. Ibid., pp. 266–67.

9. Ibid., p. 268.

10. Ibid., p. 272.

11. Ibid.

12. Ibid., pp. 276, 288.

13. Stanley F. Horn, editor, *Tennesseans in the Civil War*, pt. 1, p. 330.

14. UPM, MC 416, rolls 34 and 35.

15. Ibid., roll 73.

16. *O.R.*, vol. 31, pt. 1, pp. 623–24.

17. UPM, MC 416, roll 26.

18. *O.R.*, ser. 1, vol. 32, pt. 2, pp. 37–38.

19. UPM, MC 345, roll 131.

20. Quaife, *From the Cannon's Mouth*, p. 297.

21. *O.R.*, ser. 1, vol. 58, p. 269.

22. Quaife, *From the Cannon's Mouth*, pp. 275–76.

23. Ibid., pp. 292–93.

24. *O.R.*, ser. 1, vol. 30, pt. 4, p. 144.

25. Ibid., vol. 31, pt. 1, p. 575.

26. Ibid., pt. 3, pp. 469, 591.

27. Ibid., vol. 32, pp. 55, 416.

Colonel Stokes and his command gained a very bad reputation among the Confederates in the neighborhood for their undisciplined conduct. When Stokes died, it became a local tradition for the sons of Confederates to go to his grave and throw ice cream cones on it, saying, "There, you son of a bitch, maybe that will cool you off a little in Hell!" The custom is still observed by some of the unreconstructed.

28. *O.R.*, ser. 1, vol. 32, p. 55.

The note about the Union Negro soldiers is chilling.

29. Ibid.

Later in the war Hughes was made commander of the brigade of Bushrod Johnson and was sent to join the Army of Northern Virginia.

30. UPM, MC 416, roll 28.

31. Ibid., roll 32.

32. UPM, MC 345, roll 110.

33. UPM, MC 416, roll 34.

34. *O.R.*, ser. 1, vol. 39, p. 18.

35. Ibid., p. 353.

36. Ibid., p. 58.

37. Quaife, *From the Cannon's Mouth*, p. 295.

38. Milroy Papers, Author's Collection. This is a copy of a note in the family Bible.

39. Milroy Letters. To Mary, Jan. 1, 1865. Author's Collection. The original letters, compiled by Margaret B. Paulus, are housed in the Public Library of Jasper County, Rensalaer, Indiana. Copies of the letters can be accessed at Motlow College's Civil War Research Center, www.CWRC.org

40. Milroy Letters. To Mary, Jan. 1, 1865.

41. Milroy Papers, note in the family Bible.

42. Milroy Letters. To Mary, Jan. 1, 1865.

43. Milroy Papers, Obituary.

44. In the absence of a biography of Milroy the best available sources on the man as a general are James I. Robertson, Jr.'s *Stonewall Jackson: The Man, the Soldier, the Legend,* New York: MacMillan Publishing Co., 1997, and Donald C. Pfanz, *Richard S. Ewell, A Soldier's Life,* Chapel Hill: University of North Carolina Press, 1998.

45. Milroy Papers, Obituary in the *Republican Partizan,* Apr. 5, 1890.

46. Milroy Papers, Obituary; *O.R.*, ser. 1, vol. 21, pp. 1079–1108; Douglas Southall Freeman, *R. E. Lee: A Biography,* New York: Charles Scribner's Sons, 1934, vol. 2, pp. 482–83.

47. Milroy Letters. To U. S. Grant, May 1871.

48. Milroy Letters. To Mary, Jan. 1, 1865.

49. Milroy Letters. To Abraham Lincoln, Apr. 18, 1864; To Abraham Lincoln, Apr. 26, 1864; To U. S. Grant, May 1871; To Mary, May 20, 1864.

50. *O.R.*, ser. 1, vol. 38, pp. 179–80.

51. *O.R.*, ser. 1. vol. 39, p. 52.

52. UPM, MC 345, roll 67.

53. Ibid.

54. Ibid., roll 129.

55. Ibid., roll 215.

56. UPM, MC 416, roll 76.

Ibid., roll 81.

UPM, MC 345, roll 149.

57. *Fayetteville Times*, Apr. 15, 1915. Article on local history.

58. *Fayetteville Observer*, Apr. 6, 1919.

59. Interview with Jerry Mansfield, Historian, Lincoln County, Tennessee.

    A small marker to these three victims of the war stands on the courthouse lawn in Fayetteville.

    Lincoln County is named for General Benjamin Lincoln who received the sword of Cornwallis at Yorktown in the American Revolution.

60. *O.R.*, ser. 1, vol. 8, pp. 568–69.

61. Walter T. Durham, *Rebellion Revisited. A History of Sumner County, Tennessee, from 1861 to 1870,* pp. 190–91.

    This book contains a full description of the career of Paine while in Gallatin and provides an interesting addition to the conditions which came to exist in Tullahoma where Paine had as his commander a man of like mind in General Milroy.

62. Interview with Milan Hill, author and researcher, Tullahoma, Tennessee. Unpublished manuscript of Mr. Hill.

    Killed that night were the following men of Company A, 4th Tennessee Mounted Infantry:

    Private Berry Bruton, age 22. From Bedford County, Tenn. Buried Patrick Cemetery on Wells Hill.

    Private Sylvanus Jackson Cleek, age 20. From Bedford County, Tenn. Buried Stones River National Cemetery, Grave H. 3020.

    Private Moses C. Day, age 24. From Wilkes County, N.C.

    Private James Hashaw, age 19. From Bedford County, Tenn.

    Private John Hyde, age 26. From Bedford County, Tenn.

    Private Hillard J. Johnson, age 17. From Bradley County, Tenn.

    Sergeant Pleasant M. Melton, age 27. Previously a member of Company C, 23rd Tenn. Infantry, CSA. Buried at Stones River National Cemetery, grave H. 2907.

    Private George Ross, age 25. From Nashville, Tenn.

    Private William J. Shaw, age 23. From Bedford County, Tenn.

    Private Henry F. Sutton, age 22. Previously served in Company G, 24th Tennessee Infantry, CSA. From Bedford County, Tenn. Buried at Stones River National Cemetery, grave H. 2921.

63. UPM, MC 416, roll 27.

64. *O.R.*, ser. 1, vol. 39, p. 238.

65. UPM, MC 417, roll 77.

66. UPM, MC 345, roll 27.

67. Ibid.

68. Ibid., roll 157.

69. UPM, MC 416, roll 81.

70. Ibid., roll 42. Courtner's Mill is still a landmark on the Duck River and is today a restaurant. The Troxler family still lives in the vicinity of the Railroad Bridge over Duck River.

71. UPM, MC 416, roll 38.

72. UPM, MC 345, roll 201.

73. *O.R.*, ser. 1, vol. 32, pt. 1, pp. 101–2.

74. UPM, MC 345, roll 261.

75. Ibid.

76. Ibid.

CHAPTER 3: THE UNKNOWN FINAL FRENZY

1. Milroy Letters, To Mary, Jan 1, 1865.
2. UPM, MC 345, roll 225.
3. Ibid.
   James Edwards, the "artist," ran a photographic studio.
4. UPM, MC 345, roll 205.
5. Ibid., roll 250.
6. UPM, MC 416, roll 50.
   Moses Pittman had a large amount of shelled corn on hand because he was a distiller. One notes that he was also well armed, but that did not help him against the guerrillas.
7. Milroy Diary, entry for January 2, 1865.
8. *Fayetteville Observer*, Apr. 16, 1919. Interview with Peter Cunningham.
9. UPM, MC 416, roll 50.
   The Motley family mentioned in the list is actually the Motlow family. Lem Motlow was the uncle of Jack Daniels. At his death Lem Motlow left his distillery to his nephew. As any devotee of good things to drink knows, the distillery is still very much in business.
10. UPM, MC 416, roll 50.
    There are a total of 54 names on the list.
11. Milroy Diary, entry for Jan. 6, 1865.
12. Ibid., entry for Feb. 2, 1865.
13. Ibid., entry for Feb. 15, 1865.
14. *O.R.*, ser. 1, vol. 35, p. 118.
15. UPM, MC 345, roll 283.
16. Ibid., roll 230.
17. Ibid., roll 213.
18. Ibid., roll 297.
19. UPM, MC 416, roll 54.
20. UPM, MC 345, roll 43.
21. Ibid.
22. Ibid., roll 242.
23. "Reminiscences of the War", Agnes Lipscomb Whiteside, Special Collections Room, Argie Cooper Library, Shelbyville, Tennessee.
24. UPM, MC 345, roll 215.
25. Ibid., roll 203.
26. Ibid., roll 241.
27. Ibid., roll 276.
28. Ibid., roll 270.
29. Ibid., roll 261.
30. Ibid.
31. Ibid., roll 129.
32. Ibid., roll 43.
33. UPM, MC 416, roll 80.
34. Ibid., roll 88.
35. Milroy Diary, entry for Feb. 10, 1865.
36. UPM, MC 416, roll 46.

37. Ibid., roll 50.
38. Interview with Milan Hill, Oct. 13, 1999.
39. UPM, MC 416, roll 50.
40. UPM, MC 345, roll 135.
41. Ibid.
42. Ibid.
43. UPM, MC 416, roll 50.
44. Ibid.
45. UPM, MC 345, roll 65.
46. Ibid.
47. *Fayetteville Observer,* Apr. 6, 1915.
48. UPM, MC 345, roll 65.
49. UPM, MC 416, roll 50.
50. UPM, MC 345, roll 65.
51. UPM, MC 416, roll 130.
    The killing of the two Sanders men has been discussed earlier in connection with the orders issued by Milroy in Jan. and Feb. 1865, ordering expeditions to burn and kill in areas of Franklin and Coffee Counties.
52. *O.R.,* ser. 1, vol. 49, p. 34.
53. UPM, MC 416, roll 81.
54. UPM, MC 345, roll 83.
55. UPM, MC 416, roll 55.
56. Ibid., roll 54.
57. UPM, MC 345, roll 279.
58. Ibid., roll 288.
59. Ibid.
60. UPM, MC 416, roll 52.
61. Ibid.
62. UPM, MC 345, roll 270.
63. Ibid.
64. *O.R.,* ser. 1, vol. 39, p. 856.
65. Ibid., p. 862.
66. UPM, MC 345, roll 270.
67. Ibid., roll 248.
68. Ibid., roll 195.
69. Ibid., roll 127.
70. Ibid.
71. Ibid.
72. Ibid., roll 250.
73. *O.R.,* ser. 1, vol. 40, p. 848.
74. UPM, MC 345, roll 175.
75. UPM, MC 416, roll 64.
76. UPM, MC 345, roll 258.

CHAPTER 4: THE UNKNOWN WARRIORS

1. UPM, MC 416, roll 19.
2. Ibid., roll 21.

3. Ibid., roll 22.
4. Ibid., roll 41.
5. UPM, MC 345, roll 285.
6. Ibid., roll 40.
7. Ibid., roll 285.
8. Ibid., roll 151.
9. *O.R.*, ser. 1, vol. 40, p. 387.
10. Ibid., vol. 41, p. 203.
11. UPM, MC 416, roll 42.
12. UPM, MC 345, roll 201.
13. Ibid., roll 206.
14. UPM, MC 416, roll 58.
15. UPM, MC 345, roll 238.
16. Ibid., roll 237.
17. UPM, MC 416, roll 59.

 This record illustrates the difficulty in using the records in trying to identify proper names. The clerk who wrote this petition misunderstood the accent of the black men speaking to him. The family name is Maupin and is clearly identified in the Bedford County Census records.

 It is also common for several endorsements to be written on the back of a paper so that one can trace the chain of command as the paper makes its way from hand to hand. In this case, it is of interest to note that the petition was written, read by General Thomas' staff, passed on to two additional government agencies, and an action order was issued in the case, all on the same day.

18. UPM, MC 416, roll 59.
19. UPM, MC 345, roll 284.
20. Ibid., roll 222.
21. Ibid., roll 241.
22. Ibid., roll 66.
23. UPM, MC 416, roll 52.
24. UPM, MC 345, roll 63.
25. Ibid., roll 68.
26. Ibid., roll 126.
27. Ibid.
28. UPM, MC 345, roll 128.
29. UPM, MC 345, roll 263.
30. Ibid., roll 70.
31. UPM, MC 416, roll 56.
32. UPM, MC 345, roll 194.
33. Ibid., roll 259.
34. Ibid., roll 294.
35. Ibid., roll 156.
36. Ibid., roll 81.
37. Ibid., roll 131.
38. Ibid., roll 99.
39. Ibid., roll 30.
40. UPM, MC 416, roll 58.

41. UPM, MC 345, roll 84.
42. Ibid.
43. Ibid.
44. Ibid.
45. Ibid.
46. Ibid.
47. Ibid.
48. Ibid.
49. Ibid.
50. Ibid.
51. Ibid., roll 265.
52. Ibid., roll 299.
53. UPM, MC 345, roll 87.

Bibliography

Blakemeyer, Geoffrey. "The Pioneer Brigade." http://www.thecivilwargroup.com.

Bradley, Michael R. *Tullahoma: The 1863 Campaign for the Control of Middle Tennessee.* Shippensburg, Pa.: Burd Street Press, 2000.

Durham, Walter T. *Rebellion Revisited. A History of Sumner County, Tennessee, from 1861 to 1870.* Franklin, Tenn.: Hillsboro Press, 1999.

Fayetteville Observer. Fayetteville, Tenn. April 6, 1919. Interview with Peter Cunningham.

Horn, Stanley F., editor. *Tennesseans in the Civil War,* 2 parts. Nashville, Tenn.: Civil War Centennial Commission, 1964.

Jordan, Thomas, and J. P. Pryor. *The Campaigns of General Nathan Bedford Forrest.* New York: De Capo Press, 1996. Originally published in 1868.

Lytle, Andrew Nelson. *Bedford Forrest and His Critter Company.* Nashville: J. S. Sanders & Company, 1994. Originally printed in 1931.

McMurry, Richard M. *Atlanta, 1864: Last Chance for the Confederacy.* Lincoln: University of Nebraska Press, 2000.

Milroy Diary. Unpublished. Author's Collection.

Milroy Letters. Unpublished. Author's Collection.

Milroy Papers. Unpublished. Author's Collection.

Official Records, see *War of the Rebellion.*

Quaife, Milo M. *From the Cannon's Mouth: The Civil War Letters of General Alpheus Williams.* Detroit: Wayne State University Press, 1959.

Swint, Henry Lee. *The Northern Teacher in the South.* Nashville: Vanderbilt University Press, 1941.

Union Provost Marshal, File of Individual Citizens. Microfilm Collection. National Archives.

Union Provost Marshal, File of Two or More Citizens. Microfilm Collection. National Archives.

War of the Rebellion: A Compilation of Official Records of the Union and Confederate Armies. 128 volumes. Washington, D.C.: Government Printing Office, 1880–1896.

Whiteside, Agnes Lipscomb. "Reminiscences of the War." Manuscript in the Special Collections Room at the Argie Cooper Library, Shelbyville, Tennessee.

Wyeth, John Allen. *That Devil Forrest.* Baton Rouge: LSU Press, 1989.

Index

First names were given where known.

A

African Americans, 165
  education, 194
  occupations, 167
Anaconda Strategy, 1

B

Battle, Dollie, 149
Billings, Maj. A. W., 92, 96
  and Virginia Moore, 154
Blackmore, Dr. Jesse A., 18
Blackwell, Mrs. Mary, 84–86
Blackwell, Robert Buchanan (Captain
    Bob), 69, 80, 86
Bonner, Dr. William, 137, 185
Bonner, William, Jr., 185
Bradley, Col. Luther P., 3–5
Bragg, Lt. Gen. Braxton, 3, 34
Brixey, Capt. Calvin, 36, 111
Butts, Edward, 122

C

Camp Chase, Illinois, 22, 77
Chadd, James, 141
Chapel Hill, Tenn., 15
Chasteen, Mrs. Elizabeth, 106
Chattanooga, Tenn., 7
Cliff, Lt. Col. W. J., 132
Cowan, Tenn., 40
Cumberland, Army of the, 2
  at Chattanooga, 7
  Chickamauga, 39
  defense of N&C, 34
  make-up of, 21, 166
Cunningham, Joel, 116, 131, 134
Cunningham, Peter, 131

D

Decatur and Nashville Railroad (D&N),
  2, 10
Decherd, Tenn., 30
disloyal ladies (to the Union), 82

E

Edens, Benjamin, 190
Elk River, 29
Elkins, William, 151, 191

F

Fayetteville, Tenn., 29, 76, 104
Ferguson, Champ, 56, 161
Fletcher, J. T., 17
Forrest, Maj. Gen. Nathan B., 11
  command of 4th Alabama Cavalry, 35
Franklin, Tenn., 94, 115
Franklin County, Tenn., 30, 110

G

Galbraith, Col. Robert, 58
Gurley, Capt. Franklin (Frank), 35

H

Hibbs, Mrs. J. Gail, 154–61
Home Guards, 81, 103
  as peacemaker, 114
  revenge of, 110
Hood, Lt. Gen. John B., 94, 108
Huddleston, William, 122–31
Hughes, Col. John M., 55–57

J

Judd, Clara, 25–27

209